Nicoletto Giganti's

The School of the Sword

A New Translation

by

Aaron Taylor Miedema

With additional translations by

Tara Lynn England

and

Kim Reynolds

Illustrated by

Yvonne Rogers

Legacy Books Press Classics

Published by Legacy Books Press
RPO Princess, Box 21031
445 Princess Street
Kingston, Ontario, K7L 5P5
Canada

www.legacybookspress.com

This edition first published in 2014 by Legacy Books Press
1

Additional translations by Tara Lynn England and Kim Reynolds.
Illustrations by Yvonne Rogers.
Photographs by Bosah Vanderburg
Photographs modeled by Wayne Renaud, David Stamper, Yvonne Rogers, Erin McMorrow, Maria Meerson, and Aaron Miedema.

Printed and bound in the United States of America and Great Britain.

This book is typeset in a Times New Roman 11-point font.

Library and Archives Canada Cataloguing in Publication

Giganti, Nicoletto, active 17th century
[Scola. English]
     Nicoletto Giganti's The school of the sword / a new translation by Aaron Taylor Miedema ; with additional translations by Tara Lynn England and Kim Reynolds ; illustrated by Yvonne Rogers.

Translation of Scola overò teatro nel quale sono rappresentate diverse
     maniere, e modi di parare, e di ferire di spada sola, e di spada e
     pugnale; dove ogni studioso portrà essersitarsi e farsi prattico nella
     professione dell'armi, originally published in 1606.
Includes bibliographical references.
Issued in print and electronic formats.
ISBN 978-1-927537-07-7 (pbk.).--ISBN 978-1-927537-09-1 (kindle)

     1. Swordplay--Handbooks, manuals, etc.--Early works to 1800.
2. Fencing--Handbooks, manuals, etc.--Early works to 1800. I. Miedema,
Aaron Taylor, 1971-, translator II. Title. III. Title: School of the sword.
IV. Title: Scola. English.

GV1145.G5413 2014   796.86   C2014-900617-9
                                                   C2014-900618-7

This book denies challenging any of the books next to it to a duel to the death.

Table of Contents

Acknowledgements

I have a few people I must thank for the creation of this work.

For the interpretation of the work I must thank the members of the Cavalier Society and the Venerable Order of the Monkey for providing me the space, time, people, and intellectual banter that permitted me to construct, deconstruct, and then reconstruct my ideas on the meaning of the text.

I must also thank my partner Yvonne Rogers for her hard work on the redrawing of the original artwork that made this work possible. As well, thanks to Bosah Vanderburg for the photography to help flesh out Giganti's ideas and training exercises.

The next person is Gary Chelak who introduced me to Nicoletto Giganti in motion in Amsterdam, New York. I owe a lot to Gary for showing me some of the pointers of Giganti's system of the fence. And of course I must thank him for the appealing idea that "Giganti is fencing for lazy people."

And finally a hearty thanks to Silvia D'Onofrio who assisted in the proof reading of the work. She helped with the many of the tenses of Italian I was not familiar with, and thus rightly deserves some credit in the translation of the document. But above and beyond this Silvia worked under the duress of the tight deadline I set for myself and for which I was constantly late. Under this tight and ever-shrinking deadline, she worked miracles.

About the Author

What is known about Nicoletto Giganti comes primarily from his writings. Giganti labelled himself as Venetian; however, Piermarco Terminiello and Joshua Pandragon have found evidence that suggests his family moved to Venice from Fossombone in the Marche.[1] This offers the possibility that Giganti was not a native-born Venetian.

Giganti likely wrote *Scola overò Teatro…* (1606) and his recently rediscovered *Libro Secondo…* (1608)[2] in later life. This was the case with other masters of the early seventeenth century – Salvatore Fabris (1544-1618) was fifty-eight when he wrote his treatise, and Tom Leoni asserts Ridolfo Capoferro was fifty-six when he wrote his treatise.[3] The notion that Giganti was born sometime in the middle of the sixteenth century (sometime between 1540 and 1560) is not unreasonable, but it is unverifiable at present.

What is clear is that between 1606 and 1608 Giganti seems to have

---

[1] Nicoletto Giganti, *Libro Secondo di Niccoletto Giganti*, trans. Piermarco Terminiello and Joshua Pendragon as *The 'Lost' Second Book of Nicoletto Giganti*. (Fox Spirit, 2013), 9.

[2] The publication of Terminiello and Pendragon's monograph in the final typesetting process of this book caused my publisher no end of aggravation as I needed to revise many of my ideas.

[3] 1544 as the year of birth for Salvatore Fabris is confirmed by a number of other sources. Capoferro's birth in 1556 is speculative, Leoni is the only source located so far that ascribes this date. See: Giganti (2010), xii.

moved from Venice and the Terrafirma to Tuscany. His second book was published in Pisa and indicates that in 1608 he was the Master of Arms for the Order of San Stefano, an order of knighthood established in 1561 by Duke Cosimo de'Medici I. The dedication of the 1628 edition of Scola overò Teatro… to Duke Cosimo II suggests Giganti's association with the Medici was long lasting. This dedication also suggests that Giganti was not involved in this edition, as Cosimo II had been dead seven years; Giganti may too have died before 1628.[4]

Another work claiming to be Giganti's second book was published as a French and German translation in Frankfurt in 1622. This work resulted in a court action in which the book was accused of plagiarizing the work of Salvatore Fabris.[5] While an examination of this fake second book does bear significant similarity to Fabis' work, the fact that this second book was published again in 1644 suggests that the prosecution against the publisher may not have been successful.

What the fake second book by Giganti proves is the immense influence and popularity Giganti enjoyed as a fencing theorist. Giganti's work had considerable influence throughout western and central Europe during the seventeenth century. Giganti's work was printed more frequently than Capoferro and as many times as Fabris – more widely than Fabris, if Giganti's second book is included. He also had a wider readership; *Scola overò Teatro…* was printed in more languages than both Capoferro and Fabris. Finally, Giganti's manual (last printed in 1714) had a longer lasting success than Capoferro (last printed in 1652), and as long lasting a success as Fabris (last printed in 1715).[6]

---

[4] Giganti, *Libro Secondo…*, 11 and 13.

[5] The accusation is made in 1677 by Johann Joachim Hynitzsch in his German Translation of Salvatore Fabris. See: Nicoletto Giganti, *The School or Theatre…*, trans. Tom Leoni as *Venetian Rapier, The School or Salle, Nicoletto Giganti's 1606 Rapier Fencing Ciriculum*, (Wheaton: Freelance Academy Press, 2010), xiii and Giganti, *Libro Secondo…*, 11.

[6] There are eight extant re-printings of Giganti's first book: three in Italian (1606, 1608, and 1628), three in both French and German (1619, 1622 and 1714), and two in German (1622 and 1623). Salvatore Fabris was printed nine times during the seventeenth and early eighteenth centuries in both Italian (1606 and 1624) and German (1615, 1616, 1617, 1619, 1626, 1677, and 1713). Capoferro was published four times in Italian (1610, 1629, 1632, and 1652). Giganti, Nicolot, *Escrime Nouvelle ou Theatre, auquel sont representees diverses manieres de parer et de fraper d' espee seule et d'espee et poignard* (Jacques De Zeter, Frankfurt, 1714); Henk Pardoel, *Fencing, a Bibliography*, (Multi M/IT Publishing) http://www.fencingbibliography.com/_uk/index.html; and Scola Artis Gladii Treatise Database, http://www.middleages.hu/english/martialarts/treatise_database.php

Introduction

I have been working on the translation and interpretation of Nicoletto Giganti's 1606 rapier treatise for ten years. Much to my chagrin, Tommaso Leoni published his translation just as I began to put the finishing touches on my own. So let me explain why a second translation is worthy of publication and worthy of your time and attention. My wish is to improve the fledgling research on the topic of historical fencing, and from this perspective a second translation is required.

Simply put, all translation involves interpretation, but, Leoni has taken his interpretation of the text too far. Sometime it is simply incorrect, as seen in his translation of the title of Giganti's lesson 26. Giganti's title reads "Della Contracavatione in distantia,"[1] which Leoni has translated to mean: "Counterattack with a cavazione from out of measure."[2] Giganti mentions neither 'counterattack' (the closest word in Florio is to counter beat or buffet someone (*contrabattare*)) or 'measure' (*misura*). The literal translation is: "Of the Countercircle in distance," even the placement of the action is incorrect.

---

[1] Nicoletto Giganti, *Scola overò teatro nel quale sono rappresentate diverse maniere, e modi di parare, e di ferire di spada sola, e di spada e pugnale; dove ogni studioso portrà essersitarsi e farsi prattico nella professione dell'armi*, (Antonio et G. de Franceschi, 1606), 48.

[2] Giganti (2010), 28.

He has also altered the text in order to add modern fencing theory and techniques which Giganti did not require or intend. For example, in lesson 10 Giganti concludes with a short admonishment: *"avvertendo sempre di tener la vostra Spada fuori della vostra vita, accio non vi possa ferire."*[3] Leoni translates this as: "Also, please always bear in mind to keep your sword out of your presence, so as to remain safe."[4] The problem is word choice – nowhere in Giganti's text appears the words 'please' (*piacere*), 'also' (*anche* or *pure*), and most importantly 'presence' (*presenza*). This last word, 'presence,' is Leoni putting modern fencing terminology into Giganti's mouth, and, it requires a substantial footnote to explain what it means, even to the modern reader:

> Giganti is referring to the concept of opposition, although the specific fencing term does not appear until at least a century later. In layman's terms, this means situating your hilt and forte so as to push or exclude the opponent's point from you silhouette ("out of your presence") while you attack or counterattack. Opposition is effect by forming an obtuse angle between the sword-arm and the blade, and it is the main mechanical way to avoid receiving a hit while delivering an attack.[5]

My translation adheres more closely to Giganti's original. I have translated this sentence in the following manner: "Heeding always of holding your sword outside of your torso, so that you shall not be wounded." Giganti's original intention is clear without the imposition of modern fencing terminology.

Leoni has also altered the organization of the work and even eliminated one of the pictures. In these cases it is merely extra text. However, in other cases Leoni's imposition of modern theory actually contradicts Giganti's teaching. For example, in the first lesson on the guards and counterguards Leoni instructs that the dagger is to be pointed at the opponent's shoulder.[6] This is not what Giganti wrote. While there is a lacuna at this particular spot in the readily available online facsimile of the 1606 Italian edition, the French-German 1619 edition clearly states that the dagger is to guard the sword. Another example of Leoni's changing of Giganti's original text is found in the elimination of reference to moving the body to the inside or the outside, as such instruction contradicts both modern fencing theory and Leoni's interpretation.[7]

---

[3] Giganti (1606), 41.
[4] Giganti (2010), 12.
[5] Ibid, 12.
[6] Ibid, 2.
[7] Ibid, 15.

I hope the reader can see that my work here is a more literal translation, designed to aid readers not versed in Italian to come to their own interpretation of Giganti's system, rather than as a vehicle for my own interpretation. Although I have also offered an interpretation separate from the translation, I have endeavoured to present this work in a manner that permits Giganti's text to be used to contradict my own. This may be more difficult to read than interpretive translations, but, by doing so, the reader is given the opportunity to examine for themselves the ambiguities and complexities inherent in both the original text and the art of translation. As a result, I encourage all readers to criticize and correct my errors using the translated text I have provided.

It is important to see a work in the wider context of the field of fencing, in relation to both Giganti's contemporaries and modern theorists. Leoni certainly did this, comparing Giganti with his contemporaries Capoferro (1610) and Fabris (1606), and imposing modern theory and terminology. However, Leoni failed to let Giganti's work stand on its own merits, changing Giganti's terminology and vocabulary to that found in the works of Fabris, Capoferro, and Olympic fencing. A clear example of this is Leoni's need to explain the Agrippan system of sword guards in spite of Giganti's rejection of this system in *Scola overò Teatro*.[8] Leoni states empahtically that this was Giganti's mistake and not his own:

> There is nothing in Giganti's text that points to any substantial idiosyncrasies in the actions he presents or the mechanics he uses. What he describes is a distillation of the actions and the mechanics that can be found in Fabris, Capoferro, Alfieri and other authors of his time.[9]

Leoni's grouping of Giganti, Capoferro, and Fabris all into a single category naturally raises a question of focus. This single classification fails to acknowledge the differences in the composition and publication of the particular works. The differences between them suggest rival intellectual movements in Italian fencing. This in turn raises a question: how much of the work of other masters is it reasonable to use in the interpretation of a single work?

On the surface, the single categorization is correct – all three of these masters were proposing systems of fighting with a Rapier, and they were Italian instructors. However, this is where the similarities begin to end. The most striking difference of Giganti's system of fencing when compared to those of his contemporaries is the frugality and simplicity of Giganti's manual. The uneven printing quality and limited use of printing graphics –

---

[8] Ibid, xv-xvi.
[9] Ibid, xiv.

aside from the illustrations of fencing – suggests that Giganti's manual did not have the wealthy patronage behind it that the work of his fellow masters did. This may be evidence of Giganti's lack of capital, as he minimized the expense of printing by limiting the number of pages. This gives an unusual feel to both Giganti's work and his approach to Fencing in comparison to his contemporaries.

This suggests that there were rival schools of fencing theory in sixteenth and seventeenth century Italy, rather than a single approach to swordplay. This idea of rival theories fits well with the intellectual history of fencing in Italy. In the middle of the sixteenth century, fencing theorists began to challenge the dominance of the Bolognese, or Dardi, school of Swordsmanship. While the Dardi school remained influential in the second half of the sixteenth century, there were a growing number of new theorists who can be grouped into two groups loosely aligned with the two early challengers to the Dardi tradition.

If the extant publications are an accurate measure, the Bolognese school of fencing dominated Italian fencing in the first half of the Sixteenth Century. Beginning with an anonymous Bolognese manuscript at the turn of the sixteenth century (c. 1500), the Bolognese masters documented a consistant, complex, and broad system of martial arts that covered the use of a wide range of weapons. The Dardi system was elaborated on by Antonio Mancciolino (1531) and the highly influential Achille Marozzo (first published 1536). While comprehensive, this system of martial arts did have its drawbacks; it often lacked a clear organization and curriculum. It was also cumbersome in its terminology – for example, the Dardi system included 17 guards with the sword and buckler.

In the 1550s, two fencing theorists sought to simply the elaborate Bolognese system of guards. The first was Bolognese master Angelo Viggiani, who ran a popular fencing school in Venice. In his *Lo Schermo...* (written 1552, published 1575), he reduced the positions of the sword to twelve functionally named guards. His distinction between guards that were *perfetto* (with the tip in line to deliver the thrust) and *imperfetto* (with the tip not in line to deliver a thrust) did not influence future theorists. However, his division of guards into *offensiva* (to the outside of the fencer's body) and *diffensiva* (to the inside of the fencers body) were adopted by later theorists. Roman trained master Hieronime Cavalcabo (first published in 1595) and Nicoletto Giganti both adopted this distinction of inside and outside guards.

The other theorist of the middle of the sixteenth century who sought to streamline the Bolognese guards was the Milanese architect and mathmetician Camillo Agrippa. His *Trattato Di Scientia d'Arme...* (1553) was first printed in Rome and has had considerable long-term influence on fencing theory. Agrippa reduced the guards to four primary positions, each with a simple numerical designation. A number of fencing theorists were influenced by Agrippa; both Ridolfo Capoferro and Salvatore Fabris certainly adopted the numeric classification of guards, if not the precise positions of the guards. Agrippa's work is seen by some as a paradigm shift, but this characterization fails to separate the several concurrent innovations that Agrippa made: one is the actual guards he used, another is his numeric system of classification, a third is the use of naked figures, and so on. The work of another follower of Agrippa, Giacomo Di Grassi, highlights this point. The guards in Di Grassi's *Ragione di adoprar sicuramente l'Arme* (1570) assume similar positions to those proposed by Agrippa, but, Di Grassi rejected the numeric designation of those guards and the use of naked figures. The differences between the theorists influenced by Agrippa demonstrate that Agrippa was the source of numerous small innovations in presentation, organization, and content. The notion that Agrippa's work marked a paradigm shift in the intellectual history of fencing is also challenged by the masters who embraced the ideas espoused by Viggiani. If this were not enough, the Dardi system continued well after the 1550s. Achille Marozzo's *Opera Nova...* continued to be reprinted until 1615.[10] As well, one of Marozzo's students, Giovanni Dall'Agocchie, published a new Dardi school manual, *Dell'Arte di Scrima* (1572), at Venice.

These differences in both the content and the publication between manuals suggest structural and philosophical differences and a distinction between aristocratically fashionable and unfashionable modes of swordplay. This understanding of fashion is less about position among aristocratic society and more about the tastes of the book buying public. Giganti acquired a position as a Master of Arms for an order of knighthood; however, to printers who paid the expense for paper, ink and typesetting, the calculation of financial return on the product indicates that Capoferro and Fabris' more elaborately printed works were expected to generate a greater financial return. When the factors of Giganti's alternative system and apparent lack of capital are considered together it suggests that one may have caused the other. The seeming dominance of Agrippan theory – or at least elements of it – may have been because it was fashionable. It is possible that systems of fencing following the pattern of Agrippa had garnered a wealthier clientele.

This places the front matter of the 1619 French and German edition of

---

[10] *Opera Nova* was published in: 1536, 1540, 1546, 1550, 1580, and 1615. Henk Pardoel, *Fencing, a Bibliography*, (Multi M/IT Publishing) http://www.fencingbibliography.com/_uk/index.html and Scola Artis Gladii Treatise Database, http://www.middleages.hu/english/martialarts/treatise_database.php

Giganti in a curious light. The French publisher felt compelled to justify Giganti's system of fencing as a science of the highest order. He also acknowledged the importance of mathematical fencing espoused by Camillo Agrippa. At the same time, he emphasized that Giganti's work differed greatly from that of Agrippa. What the introduction of the 1619 edition of Giganti does tell us for certain, is that the publisher believed that the expense of composing and publishing six additional pages was a worthwhile return on his investment, and that the classification of fencing as a science had fiscal ramifications.

There are other questions that are implied by the aesthetic and broader intellectual differences between Giganti, Capoferro, and Fabris. For example, Giganti's rejection of Agrippan theory leads to questions about Agrippa's influence and uniformity within the work of all Italian fencing theorists. If Giganti could choose to use the naked figures of Agrippa but nothing else, how might other theorists like Capoferro or Fabris have altered or omitted Agrippan theory in their own works? As a result, in order to develop a proper understanding of an individual master's work, it is necessary to focus narrowly on the master's words and ideas and place them above those of the theorist's contemporaries.

To simply say that Giganti was an Italian Rapier master is inadequate, and, it also can (and has) led to serious misinterpretations of his work. The problem here is the imposition of a (for lack of a better word) *genre* in fencing. Giganti, Capoferro, and Fabris all were Italians teaching the use of the same weapon. There are similarities between the combative actions examined and their theoretical typologies. This lends itself to the identification of a genre of fencing, but too often this genre is given a universal status – as a result the *genre* can get in the way of identifying the peculiarities of the work of individual masters.

Returning to Leoni's translation of Giganti and his incorrect single categorization of Italian fencing masters. Giganti had a very different approach and action in comparison to the work of Capoferro and Fabris. I also hold that Capoferro is significantly different than the system proposed by Fabris.[11]

---

[11] Fabris is heavily influenced by the system laid down by Camillo Agrippa and seems to be using a largely unadulterated forms of his guards. This does not seem to be the case with the work of Capoferro. Capoferro adopted the basic organizational concepts of Agrippa, but, then applied this to a somewhat different set of guard positions. This is most notable in Capoferro's guard of *quarta* which is held considerably lower than that of Agrippa or Fabris. The Agrippan guard of *quarta* seems to correspond to Capoferro's transitional guard of *quarta alta* ("high fourth" in English). Upon closer inspection of the illustrations more differences between Capoferro's and Agrippa's guards begin to appear. The guard of *Terza* is also considerably different; Capoferro's being held at the same level of his *quarta*, yet, considerably higher than Agrippa's *Terza*. This is merely a brief overview of one small set

The imposition of this universal genre of Italian Rapier is demonstrated by Leoni's insistence on introducing the reader to the Agrippan system of guards. Leoni suggests that the sword is to be held in the centre of the body in the same fashion as his interpretation of Fabris. In so doing Leoni contradicts the teachings of Giganti, who admonished:

> This [the guards and counterguards] is done by taking care that his point shall not be towards the middle of your torso...

And later in the same lesson:

> You cover then the enemy's Sword with that of yours as you can see in this picture [on the guards and counterguards]. Thus, the enemy's Sword shall be outside of your torso & impossible for him to wound you...[12]

Rather than holding the sword in Agrippa's *Terza*, as Leoni proposes, Giganti instructed the hand be held – and the opponent's sword – well away from the body to the inside or outside, admonishing that to hold one's sword in the centre of the body is poor technique.[13]

Another example of letting the genre of Italian rapier take precedence over Giganti's theories is again found in Leoni's introductory notes: "Note: early 17th century Masters such as Giganti advocate performing this action with little or no pressure against the opponent's blade."[14] This statement is a direct contradiction of Giganti's advice on strong binds, angular geometry, and "affronting" the opponent's blade. Giganti frequently advocated the use of a good deal of force against the opponent's blade, both to control the opponent's sword or to force the opponent into an offensive or defensive action. Giganti in this regard, and in many others, is not easily classified as Leoni's description of a typical 'early 17th century Master;' it is also likely that the same is true of any of the masters of the seventeenth-century, or any other time for that matter.

Curiously, Leoni reconciled these contradictions between Giganti's theories and the genre of Italian Rapier by attacking the basic underpinnings of the ability of seventeenth-century books to transmit knowledge:

> The illustrations match the texts with few exceptions, which I have footnoted with my own suggestions. The greatest exception is the stance of fencers while in guard: while the illustrations depict a wide stance, the text specifies more

---

of differences between Capoferro, Fabris, and Agrippa.

[12] Lesson 5.

[13] Giganti (2010), xviii.

[14] Ibid xviii.

than once that the guard should feature a moderate stance so as to facilitate a longer lunge.

Apropros the illustrations, it has been suggested that the plates in Giganti, Capoferro and Alfieri may be variations on a common set (perhaps a royalty free set), modified ad-hoc to fit the instruction of the respective authors. This is an interesting theory, and one to which I subscribe, although as of yet I have heard nothing but mere opinion to support it.[15]

There are several problems with Leoni's claims. Firstly, Giganti was not seeking a longer lunge, he sought quickness, writing that the lunge should be: "more speedily brief than long."[16] In addition, there has been little conclusive study to determine if a modern lunge is capable of covering more distance than a Seventeenth century lunge.

A much larger issue than the length and speed of a lunge is Leoni's ideas on the stance used by Giganti. What Giganti's text specifies is: "you are to stand firm over the feet... With your torso disposed centre..."[17] Leoni has interpreted this to mean a modern stance and a modern lunge and then imposed this on his interpretation of the text, and, ignoring the illustrations as they contradict his interpretation.[18]

In order to justify this interpretation, Leoni proposes a spurious (and uncited) theory about royalty free plates for fencing manuals. Aside from the fact that there is no evidence of royalties being paid for pre-existing plates, Leoni's theory makes little logical sense when the engravers art of the seventeenth-century is considered. As yet, there has not been two different (i.e. different authors) fencing manuals with identical engravings discovered. The illustrations were commissioned and produced anew for each book. The expense to pay an engraver to make copies of royalty free pictures would have differed little from simply having the engraver make new plates specifically for the book in question. This point becomes clearer when we consider the 1619 reprinting of Giganti's treatise, if the pictures were simply decorative, why did the publisher go to the effort to make reproductions of the original plates? Why did he not simply use these supposedly royalty free plates? The answer is obvious – royalty free images and plates simply did not exist.

Aside from the logical arguments against the idea of royalty free plates, Leoni's theory is contradicted by by what we know of the engraver who made the plates for Giganti's *Scola overò Teatro*. Giganti sought out and

---

[15] Ibid, xiv.

[16] See Lesson 3.

[17] See Lesson 1.

[18] Giganti (2010), xvi and xvii.

commissioned engraver Odoardo Fialetti to illustrate his work. Fialetti was an engraver who became known for his work on anatomy, and was of sufficient skill to later be specifically sought out and commissioned by fencing master Salvatore Fabris.[19] This indicates that Giganti commissioned the illustrations of this work specifically to portray important information on his system of fencing. Giganti frequently admonished the reader to examine the pictures as part of the demonstration of his system of fencing. To suggest otherwise is to ignore the evidence Giganti himself provided, and, the current academic scholarship.

Thus the pictures provide a substantial amount of information on Giganti's techniques. When the illustrations are considered, the stance proposed by Leoni is clearly not being used. Instead, Giganti's illustrations show that the fencer's weight rests entirely, or nearly so, on the rear foot; a similar stance was proposed by Capoferro four years later.

Understanding the pictures are an accurate portrayal of the action, Giganti's advice to, 'stand firm over the feet... With your torso disposed centre...' becomes cryptic. However, the answer also lies in the illustrations and Giganti's choice to use a gridded floor. It is important to note that the point of view of the pictures is always from the side. As a result, the illustrations are capable of accurately showing the forward or backward movement of fencers, but they are not as useful in illustrating the movement to the inside or the outside. Giganti overcame this, in part, by the use of the perspective grid on the floor under the fencers. This is an intentional and purposeful choice and not a matter of convention. This grid is something not required, for example, by the more linear approach of Capoferro. The capital Capoferro invested in the elaborate landscapes for his plates clearly demonstrated that he was capable of using a gridded floor if he thought it was necessary. For Giganti, who seems to not have had the capital in the publication of his work, the use of the gridded floor was an intentional additional expense that Giganti chose to incur. Even the choices in graphics made by Capoferro and Giganti continue to suggest the dangers of identifying a single genre of Italian rapier while dismissing the importance of the illustrations out of hand.

Understanding that the gridded floor was an intentional choice on the part of Giganti, it is important to understand what information the grid was meant to convey. The grid illustrates the fencers making attacks angled to the inside and outside of the line of engagement. Thus, Giganti's true

---

[19] Laura M. Walters, "Odoardo Fialetti (1573-c.1638): the interrelation of Venetian art and anatomy, and his importance in England," (P.h.D. dissertation: University of St. Andrews, 2009), 62-65 and 86-87. Sydney Anglo, *The Martial Arts of Renaissance Europe*, (Yale University Press, 2000), 53.

meaning refers to the displacement of the body to the inside or the outside of the line of engagement. The fencer is not to lean the torso to the left or right, rather, the fencer is to displace the entire body, well balanced over the feet, to one side of the line of engagement or the other. This provides a much more consistent interpretation of all the evidence Giganti provided in his treatise.[20]

The use of angles in the attack presents another significant difference between the straight or direct line fencing techniques espoused by Capoferro. This also refutes the notion that Capoferro, Fabris, and Giganti all taught and advocated the same techniques. The knowledge of the canon of the tradition or genre of Italian rapier is useful in understanding any of the individual works. However, it can also interfere with the interpretation of individual works, as there is the temptation to impose universal definitions. What needs to be borne in mind is that masters disagreed with each other in regards to approach, theory, and method. Examine any trade, profession, or pursuit today and the same type of disagreements will be found. In these disagreements are found the motivation for each of these masters to write their own manuals and the justification for additional translations. For example, if Capoferro had thought Giganti and Fabris had defined the perfect conception of Italian rapier fencing, why was he compelled to go to the effort of writing and commissioning engravings for his own manual? When interpreting historical manuals within the larger canon of literature, the similarities are important, but so too are the differences and contradictions. To dismiss these is inadequate.

But, distinctions of fashion, classes, academics, and qualities of printing aside, Giganti provides a simple, robust, and clear system of the Fence which will prove an interesting read to anyone who has an interest in the Sword.

---

[20] This is also suggested by Florentine master Marco Docciolini, see: Marco Docciolini, *Trattato in materia di scherma* (Michaelagnolo Sermartelli, 1601)

Translation and Glossary

The intention of this translation was to render as clear an image of Giganti's words as possible, permitting the expression of all of his cleverness, simplicity, and ambiguity. I have endeavoured to accomplish this in a number of ways. I have provided the interpretation of the text separately, so that it can be investigated and disputed separately from the text of the translation. Also, The use of fencing jargon has been avoided as much as possible. Where possible, the literal translation of the Italian has been used, even if an acceptable fencing term could have been used. This prevents the bleeding over of terminology from one style, master, background, personal observation, etc... This approach mirrors Giganti's use of common parlance to describe the actions of his system of fencing. He was often inconsistent with his usages of terms – as shall be observed. This suggests that Giganti was not militant about rigidity of terms and merely used everyday language to describe the actions in his work. It is more likely the failings of the litigant age in which we live that terms have come to have such precise meanings. As well, jargon often is the creation of translation, and frequently used to maintain a hierarchical wall between master and scholar.

The following glossary provides for terms used in both the translation and the interpretation, including the case-by-case rationale for the decisions of translation that were made in the work. The primary authority used in translation is the 1611 edition of John Florio's *Worlde of Wordes*.

Affront (*Affrontare*): This is to push against the enemy's weapon in order to make him respond in a like manner, permitting an attack to be redirected, or, if the enemy does not resist then to throw the under hand thrust resolutely.

Artifice (*Artificio*): Unfortunately there is not a modern English word that translates the meanings of this Italian word well. Gary Chelak used the word "artful", while this word is grammatically simple to use; its connotation suggests "art" rather than the "illusion" and "trickery" that are wanted by both the Italian word and Giganti's usage. Tom Leoni's use of "deceitful" is closer to Giganti's intended meaning. I have chosen to use an older word – also the word chosen in the French 1619 translation of Giganti – "artifice." This often results in the use of the word "artificial." This modern connotation of "artificial" is also much closer to Giganti's intention than "artful."

Back hand blow (*Riverso*): An attack that starts from the left side (inside) of the attacker.

Bend (*Giunga*): This refers to the angle between the sword and the arm at the wrist. There is a danger when binding the opponent and throwing an under hand thrust that fencer's sword will move from the opponent's debole to their forte and fall into this angle allowing the opponent to attack around the fencer's sword.

Bind (*Stringare*): This term is often used to refer to the technique of attacking with the swords in contact. Florio gives the translation of *stringare* as "bind." I have used bind because the definitions of the word *stringare* vary greatly, even in the manuals from the first half of the seventeenth-century. Also, the use of the word bind avoids the awkward usage of the term "stringering" from *Pallas Armata* (1639).

Circle (*Cavare*): As with *stringare* the intention was to avoid the awkward use of the word "cavering" from *Pallas Armata*. Unfortunately the options in Florio are limited to terms such as "tunnelling," "cavitation," and "circle." In most modern translations *Cavare* is typically interpreted as "disengage." However, this is one of the most loaded words in fencing terminology; thus it is not used in this translation. Instead the neutral term "circle" is used to let Giganti explain his meaning in his own words.

Counter (*Contra*): This term is used in two manners. The primary meaning is that of "against," for example, a counterguard is a guard against a guard. This word is also used in the interpretation of the text to refer to an action that is intended to defeat a play or lesson. Although Giganti never referred to introducing counters specifically, he acknowledged it by his progression through what is in essence a fencing curriculum. Giganti introduces simple plays that are a valid means for dispatching an opponent. He then later introduces additional techniques which permit the fencer to counter that play if it is used against him and in turn dispatch the opponent.

Cover (*Coperto*): The ability to defend parts of the body with the Guards, although Giganti often uses the term to refer to the whole body. For Giganti, unskilled fencers are covered or uncovered, for skilled players they are covered or using artifice.

Cut (*Colpo*): Giganti gives a simple nomenclature for cutting in his system of fencing. In the *Scola overò Teatro* he simply refers to Forehand blows (*dritto*) - cuts starting from the fencer's right side, and, backhand blows (*riverso*). In both Scola overò *Teatro...* and *Libro Secondo...* these are typically aimed at the head or the leading leg. *Libro Secondo...* deals with cuts more thoroughly than *Scola over Teatro...*; the second book offers a proper cut in which the forehand or backhand blow are aimed at the neck. Giganti's statement that the forehand and backhand "attack in the form of a cross"* suggests these cuts are delivered downward at roughly 45 degrees in much the same fashion as a Squalembrato.

Debole (*Debole*): In modern fencing parlance this refers to the foible of the Sword, or half the length of the sword blade starting at the sharpened tip.

Declaration (*Dichiaratione*): the term Giganti used to describe a textual explanation.

Disorder (*Disordine*): A term that Giganti uses to refer to a situation in which a fencer is unable to easily defend him/herself. A common cause of disorder is the result of throwing the long under hand thrust.

End (*Finitmenti*): A term that Giganti used for the hilt of the sword. It may also be a specific reference to the pommel.

Feet Firm (*Piede Fermo*): This means to launch an attack and to recover to the original position held before the attack. It refers to the fencer's rear foot

---

* Giganti, *Libro Secondo*, 48.

remaining in place during the long under hand thrust and its recovery. According to Giganti, to not hold one's feet firm is to passage, to move the rear foot in front of the leading foot.

Fencer: This is a term used in the interpretation of the manual; it refers to the eventual victor in each of Giganti's lessons.

Fore hand blow (*Dritto/Mandritto*): An attack or cut that starts from the right side (outside) of the attacker.

Forte or Strong (*Forte*): As in the modern usage, forte refers to the half of the sword, lengthwise, starting at the pommel. However, in cases where forte is not used to refer to the nomenclature of the weapon it has been translated as "strong" or "strength." The retention of the fencing term "forte," meaning the rear half of the blade, has been for the sake of clarity of text.

Furnishing (*Fornimenti*): Giganti uses this term to refer to the hilt of the sword or sometimes to refer to where an opponent has placed his sword.

Increase (*Crescere*): A movement towards the enemy by stepping, or pushing with the hands or body.

Inquartata (*Inquartata*): This directly translates to "into the quarter." The quarter is never defined by Giganti, but, its usage in the text refers to moving the inside foot ahead of the outside foot and moving the body diagonally forward, either to the inside or the outside. From this usage the quarter likely comes from a division of the ground around the fencer divided by a line dividing forward and back and another dividing inside and outside, the cross lays where the fencer stands and divides the area around the fencer into four quarters. Thus, any movement not directly forward, back, inside, or outside would be a move into a quarter.

Inside (*Dentro*): Because Giganti does not deal with left-handed combatants, "inside" means towards the left side. However, for a left-handed fencer "inside" would be to the right side.

Leaning (*Appogiare*): Leaning is similar to affronting, binding, and warding. Leaning on the sword is another manner to move the offending tip away from the fencer's body by pressing the fencer's sword against the opponent's sword.

Lesson (*Lezione*): A lesson is one of the names given to a body of text under a heading. Giganti unfortunately lacks the organizational structure of other manuals of the early seventeenth-century. He failed to provide tables of contents, chapters, or any other system of numeric ordering. However, in the text there was supposed to be a numeric ordering in the original 1606 edition. There are numerous references to "picture num[ber]...." Unfortunately the numbers were never added. There may have been a problem in the printing process that led to the numbers not being included. Another possibility is that Giganti may have left the numbers out in order to encourage the reader to hire his services as an instructor. The numbers were included in the 1619 French translation, and those numbers have been included in this work.

Line of Engagement: This is not a term used by Giganti in his treatise; rather, it is a modern fencing term used in the interpretation of Giganti's system of fencing. In brief, the line of engagement is the line that can be drawn between the inside heels of the two opposing fencers. Also, the line of engagement changes moment to moment and will need to be reconsidered within each time of a fight. This concept is significant to Giganti's system as his footwork involves stepping off of this line of engagement.

Measure (*Misura*): Giganti explains clearly what this is: simply, the range at which one fencer can hit another. However, what is sometimes not clear is that – for Giganti – it is a very specific point. This differs significantly from many systems of fencing that use various measures in their analysis of combative motion. In Giganti's system of fencing, there are three places one can be in relation to the measure: outside of measure, where one is safe; in measure, where the under hand thrust can be thrown; and inside of measure which indicates that a fencer is in peril or going to the press.

Opponent: This is a term used in the interpretation of the text; it refers to the combatant that loses the exchange in Giganti's lessons.

Outside (*Fuori*): There are three common meanings for this word in Giganti's work. The first usage refers to keeping the enemy's point away from the body, toward the inside or outside as the case may be. The second usage refers to being outside of the measure, meaning out of range of the enemy's long underhand thrust. The last and most common meaning is directional. Giganti does not discuss left-handed combatants; as a result this term refers to the right side of the fencer or weapon being referred to. However, for a left-handed person "outside" would mean to the left side.

Over hand thrust (*Imbroccata*): According to Florio it is "a thrust over the opponent's dagger." Some fencing masters suggested that it was a thrust over the opponent's sword, and others an overhand thrust. Giganti's does not give a clear definition of the term. So this last definition of over hand thrust has been used to provide the greatest leeway for possible interpretation.

The over hand thrust

Passage (*Passata*): The conventional translation is to "pass" with the inside foot forward ahead of the outside foot. However, this is not an option presented in Florio or any other dictionary that was consulted. It translates directly as "stepped," or, "passage," as in a journey. This later translation is the preferred one in order to distinguish it from other stepping, and, can be used in the present tense.

Phase: This is a term used by the interpretation to examine and describe the individual elements of action used within a single time. The most significant example is the long under hand thrust, while only taking one time it consists of six consecutive actions, or phases.

Picture (*Figura*): This is the primary division of Giganti's work, although his use of this system is not consistent. For instance, some lessons have two pictures and other lessons have none. The 1619 edition used the pictures as the basis of its chapter and numeric organization. For the sake of easier textual reference this work has been organized by lesson instead of by picture.

Play: This is a defined chain of actions between fencer and opponent that follow each other to a successful resolute hit.

Point (*Punta*): This refers to the offensive tip of the sword; however, often – in fencing circles – the word *punta* is also used to refer to a thrust that comes from below shoulder level from the outside (*punta*) or from the inside (*punta riverso*). However, this is not an option that is found in Florio. For the sake of accuracy of translation this loaded meaning has been ignored and *punta* has been translated strictly as "point".

Press (*Presa*): is a term used in early modern Italian martial arts systems to refer combat at close range involving dagger fighting or grappling.[*]

Pulse (*Polso*): This is a term that refers to the underside of the wrist where the pulse is found. It is used to define hand position, for example, "turn the pulse up." Giganti's usage of the pulse is unusual, most fencing masters of the vintage referred to the palm of the hand or occasionally the finger nails.

Resolute (*Risolute*): a term used to denote an attack thrown to completion that hits the opponent. It is the opposite of a feint, which is an attack meant to draw out a defensive response.

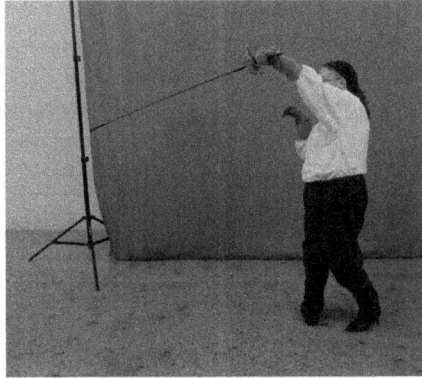

Reunite: A term taken from other fencing theory. This is to bring the leading foot back to or past the rear foot (see illustration on page xxvi). Gignati describes this action in use, but, he does not have a specific term for it. The use of the term reunite is only found in the interpretation of Giganti's plays.

Reunite, before   *Reunite, after*

Set (*Mettere*): The term is used by Giganti to refer to a fencer assuming a guard.

Side (*Banda*): Siding is the use of the "bend" of the sword to be able to make an attack around an opponent's counterguard. Giganti only uses this

---

[*] For an example of an Italian system of "Presas" see Achille Marozzo, *Arte Dell Arme di Achille Marozzo, Ricorretto, et ornate di nuove figure in rame*, (Venice: Antonio Pinargenti, 1568), chapters 168 to 273.

manoeuvre with a radical step to the side, and a dagger to control the opponent's sword.

Sword, parts of: see: Debole (*Debole*), End (*Finitmenti*), Forte or Strong (*Forte*), Furnishing (*Fornimenti*), Point (*Punta*), and True edge (*Filo dritto*).

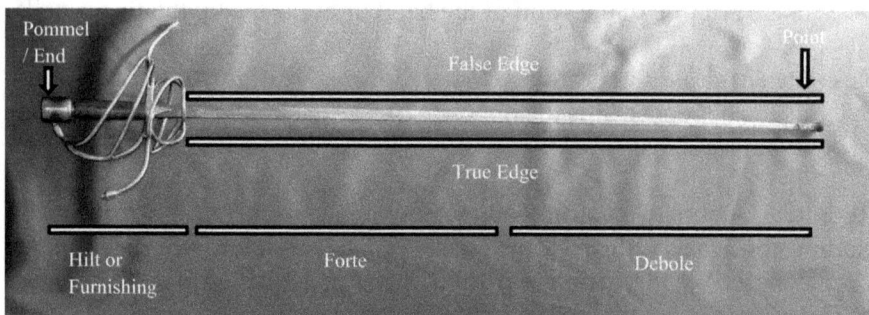

Sword nomenclature

Throw (*Tirare*): In many modern translations this word is often translated as "attack." However, this is not an option in Florio. Even modern dictionaries do not prominently list the translation of *tirare* as "attack." Instead, the word's meaning generally involves a sharp sudden movement. Also, Giganti used the word to refer to numerous things besides the sword. To encompass Giganti's varied usage of the word the neutral term "throw," from Florio, has been used.

Time (*tempo*): This is not understood in such rigid terms as it is today in the age of chronometers. Time refers to the length of time it takes for something to happen. It is not a constant factor and varies given the action being performed to describe it. The time can be altered further by the intensity and rhythm of the combatants. See Giganti's second lesson "Of the Time and the Measure."

Torso (*vita*): *Vita* is a flexible term in Italian; it can mean life, body, waist, and torso. But, Giganti's meaning can be determined by a process of elimination. He uses the term *vita* as a target in fencing, thus he refers to a physical location, ruling out "life." He also uses other terms to refer to the body and the waist. As a result torso is the remaining interpretation.

True edge (*Filo dritto*): The true edge is defined by the edge of the sword around which a fencer has wrapped their index finger and middle finger, or it is defined by the knuckle bow if the sword has one.

Uncovered (*Discoperto*): This term refers to areas that are not directly covered defensively by the sword or dagger. There are two different reasons for being uncovered, one is poor technique or being in a situation that leaves the fencer disordered, the other is for a fencer to intentionally uncover part of the body in order to use Artifice.

Under hand thrust (*Stoccata*): Florio translated this word as "Stoccata" showing that the term was in common parlance in England at the time Giganti was writing. Florio also translates it as: "a thrust, a stocado, a foyne." None of these clearly describes Giganti's *stoccata lunga*. Rather, the translation choice was determined by the translation of *imbroccata* as "over hand thrust." Giganti declares that this long underhand thrust formed the basis of all the lessons in the book, he makes little reference to different types of attacks (Over hand thrust being the exception). It should be assumed the long underhand thrust is to be used unless otherwise stated.

Wound (*Ferire*): In modern translations the word "attack" is often used; however, this is not one of the options in Florio. The term "wound" is in Florio, and capably assumes the place of the word "attack." "Wound" also gives a constant reminder of the mortal nature of the lethality of the action. It will help to note that Giganti has two categories of wounds. The first and most usual is "resolute," the other is the "feint."

School or Theatre

In which the diverse manners and ways of warding and wounding of the single Sword. And with Sword and dagger: are represented to you.

Which must be studiously carried to exercise, & to be practically done in the profession of arms.

Written by Nicoletto Giganti, Venetian.

Introduction to the 1619 Edition
Translated by Tara Lynn England with assistance from Dr. Laura Kuzmenko

To the reader
Friendly reader, how many others except the author, wanting to write about the use of arms, make no mention of what a science is. So, it seemed to me a necessary thing to say something & show its authority & with what name it is ornamented, in order that each may learn its greatness, dignity, & importance.

So first, in order that the admirers of this very noble science may be informed, before discussing and practicing these very learned and easy lessons of this valorous & experienced professor Nicoletto Giganti, I wished to make some small statements. And to observe the general rules and precepts of those, who want to investigate something. I will begin with the definition. From there will come to the general division of the word science, from which two things become much easier to understand about it, that in this beautiful science is proposed to us. Now, science is a certain and manifest experience of things acquired by learning.

There are two sorts, that is to say the speculative & practical. The speculative is a simple action of learning, according to its own object. The practical consists of the actual actions of learning. The speculative is divided into two parts, that is to say, the real speculative, & the rational speculative. The real observes the reality of its object, that which shows its nature on the outside. The rational stops at the border of these things that are governed by learning & go no further than its essence extends.

Physics is a real speculative science, which only looks at moving and natural things, like the elements. Mathematics is also a real speculative science, that which is limited to quantities, either continuous or finite. The continuous are the lines, circles, & surfaces; therefore they are measured by Arithmetic. Grammar, rhetoric, poetry, logic, etc.... are real speculative sciences.

The practical sciences are also divided in two, in the manner of the Active and the Factitive. The Active comprises the ethical, political, and economical. The Factitive is divided into seven others named: mechanics, [lacuna], agriculture, military, mercenary soldier, navigation, medicine, hunting, and the art of building.

But now to come to what I promised above, regarding this noble science. I will discourse on its qualities & nature, to see if it is a speculative or practical science. And to be brief, I say and prove with many reasons, that it is a speculative science. Without a doubt, to be a science, it cannot be acquired, except through the means of the use of learning, from which it takes its origin and birth. It is certain, to be speculative means that it does not consist of things other than the simple experience of the object, as I will show later. The objective of this science is none other than warding and hitting, the science of these things is a work of learning. Also you cannot be a professor of this science before you have experience in these two things, of which something must be known. If he is without knowledge of the times, measures, feints, circling, or resolute points, all of which all are parts of understanding, that do not extend beyond the proposed end, which is to hit and ward well. But, let us see if it is real speculative or rational speculative. I found that it cannot be rational. The reason that confirms it to me is in the manner in which it is a work of learning, ever increasing on what came before. Therefore, we have to believe it is real speculative. We say real, because the experience of the end is demonstrated to us externally through the learning: more than knowing how to hit & ward: with time and measure; in feints, circling and resolute strikes. How many of these are works of learning, we cannot experience them all but externally, consisting of the carriage of the body & sword in guards & counterguards. Things that consist of circles, angles, lines, surfaces, measures and numbers, of these, as they can be observed, we can look to the writings of Camillo Agrippa & many other teachers of this science. But, note well, that while these works of learning cannot demonstrate themselves without an external operation; so we cannot experience the external operation, without the first works of learning. Of the kind we cannot experience except that this science comes from learning, if not from the exterior. Moreover, the exterior cannot itself be experienced without the work of learning. These works, to demonstrate the greatness, excellence & perfection of this profession, will be found always joined. Like we will never have the sun without the day or the day without the sun, so never will these works be separated. It is left for us to see what kind of real speculative science it is. I say furthermore, that it is a real speculative science, mathematical, of geometry & arithmetic. Of geometry because it consists of lines, circles, angles, surfaces and measures. Of arithmetic because it contains also certain numbers. And there is no movement of the body which does not make an angle or a circle: nor movement of the sword which does not follow the path of a line. Nor is there guard or counterguard that is not ruled by numbers: the observation of all this which all depends on the learning of the times and the measures. Therefore I conclude that this very noble science is real speculative, mathematical, of geometry & arithmetic, like was said above.

But a curious person could answer to me about the above, that the science of arms is more properly a practical science, for the very reasons I alleged above. Where I say, a practical science does not only depend on the experience of its own object, but also on the way it works. The sword science, is a science not only powered by the experience, but also principally by the working. To say it properly, it then follows that it is a practical science and not speculative. To this objection I answer, that all things have some natural workings, and, all workings are of three types. Because some are interal. These have there being in pure & simple learning & come from a rational speculative. Others are interal & external. These having their being inside & outside of learning & come from a real speculative. Others are simply external. These have their being only outside of learning and depend on a practical science, being either active or factitive. The real speculative factitive science is no different than the practical, except for the real speculative; how many would work on the exterior of their object, always restraining the experience received in learning. The practical science, outside of which it cannot work, except outside of its object; it could also come to experience of itself if not externally. The science of arms, often working externally, therefore, cannot ever be said to be practical, because it is a real speculative science having the experience of its object in learning.

We have therefore shown what is this science, similar to Mathematics of geometry & arithmetic, consisting of numbers, lines, & measures. Of these, the author makes no mention in his observations, to that end not only the learned persons, but, also the mighty unlearned harvest more fruit. These lessons and drawings show how we can experience the times, measures, circlings, feints, & resolutes, to be able to ward and hit with advantage, without the working descriptions of the many lines, circles, angles, & surfaces, that can often confuse and delay the reader more than they can advance.

As for the circles, lines & other things mentioned above, the studious and diligent lover will easily come to experience through practice. In my opinion, I admonish everyone who wishes to give themselves over to this exercise, that they begin by the study of good writings. Because, he who will study by experience will have things important to this art, advance in less time, & become more perfect in all the required particularities, than he who has not studied. How much could he have also learned if he had given more time & practice? Always his experience will be well founded.

For the rest: what is the dignity & consideration of this profession? What comeliness and grace does it require? What reputation and honour is it due? &, finally what is the responsibility of the person who carries a sword & makes it his profession? It is said regarding the dignity and consideration, that everything derives of these qualities from experience, which we come to by dividing it. So the science of the sword is divided into three parts. The first is divided in two – that is to say, in natural and artificial. The natural one is a demonstrative discourse, of which man makes natural use of warding or of hitting, seeking by his own learning the means of governing nature in order to make his defence and attack to his enemy. We often see this experience in a courageous man, who in a quarrel comes up against someone with the reputation of a great master in this art.

Artificial is the one that, with learning and practice understands under certain rules the ways of knowing how to ward and hit without danger with time and measure: so that when the man falls into a fight, he uses the true ways of protecting his person. These two qualities the author shows a very great experience of, so that the reader will find himself to be entirely satisfied.

The second part is this, mainly the artificial science of the sword divides in two: in demonstrative & practiced. The demonstrative is this: it demonstrates the true way of knowing how to ward and hit, with feet firm or passaging, and, when we need to engage the enemy or retreat, by these lines, circles, & circumstances mentioned above. Those by which learning will govern itself & includes diverse postures and counter postures of the body. The practiced one is the same as the demonstrative, which acquired is applied to the understanding of a few meanings. There is no difference between them, except for the demonstrative is a part of itself, and the practice is used in the understanding of many things.

The third part is this: that the demonstrative science of the sword is once more divided in two: the first demonstrative is made up of compound terms. That is to say, composed of simple terms, which contain many other terms, themselves demonstrative of many circumstances, like being outside of measure, with open arms, the weapons high or low. There are called simple terms, that is to say, terms not learned by the enemy. They are also called simple because they are natural & composed because they have diverse considerations. These are divided into firsts & in seconds. The first, are the conceptions of real things learned through learning, for example, warding and hitting. Those are of first or principal intention. The seconds are the conceptions formed of learning. These are the second intention, which is the knowledge of warding and hitting, which precedes from the first. Considering the learning, having included the craft of warding and hitting, discussed like this it can be constructed in diverse manners. The second demonstrative consists of complex terms, which is to say, of terms which take in themselves many simple demonstrative terms. The craft which we seek, these terms are united in measure or separated in distance and shown such as: being on guard, barred in arms shown either in distance, measure, posture, or counter posture of the body. These are the things that we able to work through. So we see by the qualities & terms of which it is comprised this so beautiful science .

In this manner it is of great dignity. Being real speculative mathematical of geometry and arithmetic & containing within itself remarkable parts. Therefore, I say it requires a great seemliness and reputation. This is demonstrated by the fact this science is found principally in courts of royalty and princes, & in greatly renowned and famous cities: where it is studied & practiced by Barons, Counts, Knights, & other people of great quality.

For no other reason than it is ennobling, exciting, & enflames the spirits to great things, heroic acts, & enterprises. Because, each and every one desires to demonstrate the virtue of his spirit, value, & strength of the body, &, the gallantry & dexterity of his person. It always requires an amiable equality & will not suffer any wrong or outrage. It desires to be known and learned: but will not show its purpose at any light occasion. It avoids contention with vile persons. It does not always do all it can, but, shows itself in the right time and place. It avoids drunkenness, makes few speeches, travels with gravity, & a nimble eye. It loves honorable custom, & is of amiable & noble conversation. Here in regard of the seemliness & reputation of this science.

In regard of the honour that it is due, it must be advised that the observation of all the things just said give to the honour to it. It leaves only to say that it is the obligation of the person who carries the sword. We will not make mention here of those common and somewhat infamous duelists. Those who have mislearned this profession, and also have little honour. Being reduced to a very poor and miserable state, they have not only abandoned all the virtue required in a noble science, they are distanced from all human discourse. They also reject the fear of God, burying themselves in their unhappy designs and so they do not make use of these other things, to their ruin and condemnation.

Therefore friendly readers, the obligation of anyone who so practices, is to be served on four occasions. Firstly, for the faith. Secondly, for the country. Thirdly, for the defense of oneself. Finally, for the maintenance of honour. It should never be applied for wrong or injustice and only for the defense of a just cause. He who portends to defend an unjust cause causes injury to this profession. He will never allow a good man, to be forced to intermix himself in some unjust quarrels, but, will willingly hazard forth for the defense of justice & principally in the occurrences discussed above. Furthermore, it ought to be some just occasion or reason. For, to fight without reason is the act of fools and drunkards.

There are others, who having acquired some beginning of this science put the sword at their side & make a thousand insolent remarks to stop, irritate, and wound; seeking to kill sometimes a passerby. They believe that this is a way to acquire a reputation or to become feared. But, they are greatly wrong, because over those who do great wrong by this art, that which should never be deployed without reason, they offend God & will not acquire other things than a just hatred from God & men. To not bore the reader, I will be no longer, only I exhort the noble spirits to take heed of the very beautiful lessons & observations of our author. To practice diligently, confident that they will profit in a short time They should guard against abuse and only to behave in the manner that has renown and honour.

Lesson 1: The Guards and Counterguards

Anyone who wants to be a professor of the science of Arms, it is necessary for you to know many things. Thus, I give these my principle lessons, I begin with the guards & counterguards, meaning the postures and counter postures of the Sword. Because, it is from these that every fight begins, it is necessary to know these first, in order to be able to counter the enemy safely.

As you see in my pictures, there are many things that one must take care to observe in order to be able to put oneself on guard. You are to stand firm over the feet, for these are the base & foundation of all the body. A proper step for you to be able to increase, more nimble than wide so you may increase to attack long. You must hold the Sword & the dagger strongly in the hands. The Dagger extended either high or low; the Sword either high or low to the right side of the body always extended wide in action, wardings, and wounding. So that if the enemy throws either with the point, or edge you are to be able to ward and wound in the same time. With your torso disposed nimbly, because wanting disposition & swiftness of that, the enemy shall easily bring you to disorder with a fore hand blow, back hand blow, point, or in other manners. Without strength in this you will lie in danger. It will help you if your dagger guards the enemy's Sword, for, when the enemy throws to parry with that. That the sword is always aimed for the enemy's uncovered parts so that your adversary will surely be wounded. All this is the art of the profession.

Moreover it must be kept in mind that all the motions of the Sword are a signal to those who know how to decipher them. You must practice all the guards well; as you should not desire to encounter without these motions or guards. For, to not know how to use them, nothing will be done well. This profession requires none other than science & practice. This practice is the mistress of science. Artifice is to place yourself uncovered in guards, this is done so the enemy will place himself in disorder by throwing his sword & he will lay in peril. It is as important to place yourself under defense with cover and artifice. When the enemy binds to be able to wound you, in whatever manners he intends, you must understand what each guard avails you & know this. To one who is without this understanding & knowledge, no guard has value. This is what the guards are.[*]

One whom is aware of this profession, will know the counterguards. He will never put himself in guard, but, to prepare against the guards. This must be heeded, to understand how to set against the guards, it is best to set to this outside of measure. That is to say in distance with the Sword. The dagger up, strong in the torso & with the firm and strong step. Then you may consider the enemy's guard. Then you may go straight and smooth with your Sword securely binding his, that is to say leaning your Sword against his, thus you cover his and so it is impossible for him to wound you without circling his Sword. The reason is this, when you circle there are two workings; first to circle, behold the first time, then to wound, behold the second. In that same time while he is circling he stands to be wounded by you in many ways, as shall be seen in the pictures of my book. You should have the first time as the time of wounding. In all variety of guards it behoves your success to counter the guard with the Sword in front and with the dagger out always securing his Sword. Thus, he will always be forced to circle the sword in his first time, and he shall stand to be wounded. Nor is it possible for him to wound you, without using two times; you shall very easily protect yourself from this. This is what the guards, and counterguards are.

One of the challenges of interpreting period texts is in determining what knowledge the author took for granted – often this can be very basic information. Giganti, like so many of his contemporaries, never stated how the sword is to be held in the hand. This very basic idea seems to be an appropriate place to begin the interpretation of Giganti's text. Common

---

[*] This is an important linguistic point, English is one of the few European languages that does not make the distinction between theoretical or reported knowledge ("sapere") and practical or witnessed knowledge ("capire"). Fencing according to Giganti requires both.

modern consensus and practical application indicates that Giganti advocated placing the index and middle finger over the quillions along the true edge of the sword.

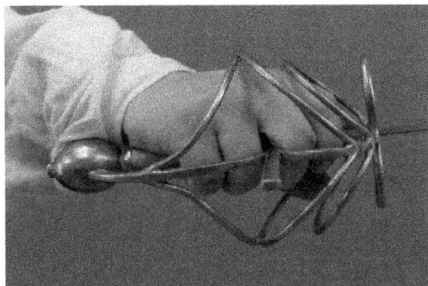

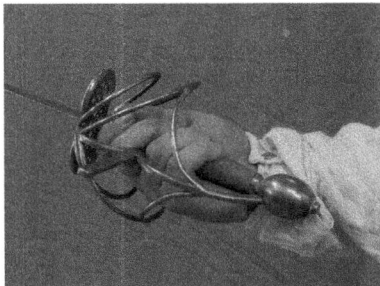

Lesson 1 is intended to refer to the entirety of Giganti's work. As a result, the breadth of this lesson may create some confusion for readers new to historical fencing or the interpretation of historical manuals. Primarily, this emanates from Giganti's inclusion of the use of the dagger in this lesson. It is worth noting that Giganti is not the only fencing theorist to make this choice; Ridolfo Capoferro also illustrated his basic guards with sword and dagger, rather than including additional pictures of the guards with the single sword.* This seems to have simply been a decision based on limiting the length of the manual and number of illustrations and thus the expense of publication. For other theorists with greater financial backing, like Salvatore Fabris, there were separate illustrations and descriptions of the guards with the single sword and those of the sword and dagger.

This lesson is important for those studying the sword and dagger techniques, and, will need to be referred back to, as Giganti does not repeat these ideas in his later lessons. In Lesson 4, Giganti makes it clear that the inclusion of secondary weapons (dagger, target, or round buckler) should not alter the basic techniques of swordplay, and they merely expand upon the techniques of the single sword.

For those studying the techniques of the single sword, the references to the dagger should be ignored. However, this does mean some alteration of the positioning of the inside hand. The illustrations will give some guidance on the positioning and posture of the inside hand in the single sword techniques. According to Plates 2 and 3, the inside hand can be held in a variety of manners, from as far back as behind the head to as far forward as the elbow of the outside arm in guard. It is unclear whether the

---

* Ridolfo Capoferro, *Gran Simulacro Dell'Arte e Dell'Uso Della Scherma*, (Siena: Salvestro Marchetti e Camillo Turi, 1610), 44-47.

particular positions of the inside hand have any particular relation to the guards that they are illustrated with.

The hand position that I favour, is that of the left figure in Plate 2. The inside hand should come to eye level. The inside shoulder should be brought forward so that the inside elbow comes to rest on the inside breast and belly of the fencer. This positioning reduces the fencer's profile to the inside and the distance that the sword has to travel in order to defend the entire body. This in turn reduces the amount of time, strength, and speed required to defend. This leaves the fencer a greater capacity to alter the movement of the sword and respond to particular situations.

This positioning of the inside hand provides an additional defense. By simply straightening the inside arm the fencer can make a broad circular downward parry, covering the majority of the torso. This simple parry is fast due to the effect of gravity on downward movement. This motion is also instinctive in the face of the threat of an incoming point.

A final note of the positioning of the hand, the fingers should be held loose and relaxed. This permits a blow that does hit the hand to pass between the fingers with far less force than if the fingers are held tightly together. For the modern fencer this will help to minimize potential injury, and for the period fencer it would minimize the chance of fingers being severed.

Giganti only makes general reference to the guards themselves in this lesson, discussing them in more detail in Lesson 5. Instead, he introduces some thematic concepts that pertain to the entirety of the treatise, and, although they seem understated, they are of critical importance in putting Giganti's techniques into practice. One significant theme is that the sword is to be held well forward of the fencer at all times. This serves several functions. First, the sword becomes a larger defensive impediment the closer it is held to the enemy. Secondly, this reduces the amount of distance, and thus time, required to hit the opponent with the sword. Ideally, the difference between the defensive and offensive positions of the sword should only be two or three inches. The simple thrust by extending the arm was not used as an attack in Giganti's system of fencing. The arm is largely meant to form a solid structure whereby the weight of the body is used to deliver the force of the attack.*

---

*Giacomo Di Grassi, *Ragione di adoprar sicvramente l'arme si da offesa, come da difesa, con un trattato dell'inganno, & con un modo di essercitarsi da se steff, per acquistare forza, giudicio, & prestezza*, (Venice: Giordano Ziletti & Co, 1570), 64-65 and Giacomo Di Grassi, *His True Arte of Defence Showing how a man without other Teacher or Master may safelie handle all sortes of Weapons*, trans. I. G. Gent, (London: I. I., 1594), page I.

Outside guard from the front   Inside guard from the front

Another theme introduced in this lesson, and perhaps the most understated, is on the placement of the fencer's feet and weight. Giganti's admonishment that 'you are to stand firm over the feet' *is of the utmost importance to the techniques included in* The School or Theatre... *This admonishment indicates that whatever posture of guard is held the fencer requires balance. What Giganti does not mention in the text is where the feet and the weight are supposed to be placed. When in guard the fencer carries their weight almost entirely on the rear leg, permitting the torso to be positioned further back, away from the threat of the opponent's sword. When throwing the long under hand thrust (see Lesson 3) the weight is transferred forward; the motion of the weight moving forward provides much of the force required in binding and striking the opponent. The transfer of weight back to the rear foot (after the attack) returns the fencer to guard. Giganti's footwork relies upon stepping off the line of engagement to the inside and outside. Thus, Giganti's admonishment on not inclining the torso is a warning that one is to execute movements to the inside or outside of the fight with the feet.*

Also contained in this lesson is the basic framework of the concept of Time and the principles of the first two plays of Giganti. Before attempting to practice the techniques contained in this lesson, lessons 2 through 8 need to be consulted. These cover the techniques required and develop these plays more thoroughly. Giganti's point is that these elementary plays of his system of fencing should be thoroughly mastered and frequently used.

Finally, in this lesson Giganti introduces the concept of Artifice. This is a more advanced concept in Giganti's system of fencing, and he does not mention this concept in practice until lesson 11. Artifice means that the fencer holds an intentionally inadequate guard in order to induce their opponent to make an attack, which is then countered by the fencer. Ideally, the opponent is then dispatched. The concept of artifice permits Giganti to maintain the simplicity of his system by having only two simple guards and to classify all others as artifice.

Inside and outside lines of attack

Lesson 2: The Time and Measure

Without the knowledge of the time & measure, one cannot know how to set in guard or counterguard; nor know how to throw the point, over hand thrust, fore hand or back hand blow; nor know what to do with the wrist; nor carry the body well; nor how to best dominate the Sword; nor is able to speak of knowing how to recover & wound. These are good for warding & wounding, lacking understanding of this, you cannot claim to know warding and wounding; because in the warding as in the wounding you would err greatly & incur a thousand perils. Having dealt with the guards and counterguards, it now lies to deal with time & measure, knowing this accommodates your knowledge of what is needed to ward and wound.

Hereafter, the measure means that you are able to arrive at the enemy with the Sword. If you cannot, it means you are outside of measure. The time is understood in this way: if the enemy is in guard, it is best you set yourself outside the measure & to go with your guard secure to the enemy's Sword with yours & understanding what you want to do. He will have to circle it, in that circling you are able to wound him. This is one time, the changing of his guard, while he is changing it is a time. If he circles, it is a time. If he comes to bind in measure, while he steps forward to arrive in measure, this is one time to wound him in the instance in which he is throwing with you warding and wounding in one time. All of this is a time. If the enemy is standing waiting firmly in guard, you go to bind him and as you are in measure you throw where he is uncovered, this is one time to wound him. This is because any motion of Dagger, Sword, feet, & body, as changing of guards, this is a time to wound. All manners of these things have times; thus they have diverse intervals. Without a doubt it behoves you, while the enemy is doing any of these motions, to then attack to wound. For while he is moving, he is not going to wound you. This is necessary to know for you to be able to wound & ward: which, as you will see in my pictures, will be demonstrated at more length.

There are a number of important concepts that Giganti covers in the second lesson. The first is that without a sense of time Giganti's teachings will be difficult to master. Another concept is that a single time equates to the amount of time taken to perform an action. The next is that, as a result, time does not have a perfect definition; rather, it is defined by the action it describes. Finally, Giganti gives the advice that the ideal time to attack is when the opponent is engaged in some action other than an attack.

There are some interesting ideas implied by Giganti's second lesson. First is that each time has a definitive beginning and end, and the transition between two times, or movements, can be interpreted as a pause or rest. This permits an understanding of the overall fight as a series of times and pauses. While Giganti himself does not state this idea directly, it is certainly one of the meanings contained in the Italian word "tempo." Regardless the musical analogy will help in understanding and finding the time in practice. This musical analogy can also be used to imply that the tempo can also be altered by the pace at which the fencers conduct their actions, although Giganti advises a slower approach in order that a fencer may: "understand… what [they] want to do."

Lesson 3: The Way of Throwing the Under Hand Thrust

Plate 1

Now that we have dealt with the guards, counterguards, measure, and times, it is necessary to show & give an understanding of how you are the carry the torso for throwing the under hand thrust safely. If you want to learn this art it follows it is necessary you must first know how to carry the torso & to throw the long under hand thrust, which can be seen in this picture. All of this lies with throwing the long under hand thrust nimbly, strongly, & quickly, then recovering backward outside of the measure. To throw the long under hand thrust, it behoves you, to be able to increase, to place yourself with a proper step. Strong, more speedily brief than long, &, in throwing the under hand thrust lengthen your Sword arm and to incline your knee as much as you are able. The true way of throwing the under hand thrust is, beforehand, when you are set in guard, it behoves you to throw the arm first. Then increase forward with the torso in one time. Thus, when the under hand thrust arrives, the enemy is unaware. If you carry the torso forward first, the enemy will be aware. Thus saved by having time to recover & will wound you in one time. Recovering backwards, it behoves you to carry the head backwards, then, after the head, follows the torso backwards & then the feet. For to carry the feet backwards first, leaving the head & torso forward, leaves you in great peril. To desire to learn this art well, it behoves you to first exercise throwing the under hand thrust. To know this you will more easily learn the rest, as not knowing will be the contrary. Take care gentlemen readers, you need to always remember my second lesson upon the time in this way of throwing the under hand thrust. This picture gives better understanding to the lesson, which, will not be ill to say, put these things in your mind.

The first three phases of the long under hand thrust

Giganti's lunge is meant to be a rapid comfortable attack rather than one seeking to gain as much range as possible, or in other words, fluidity of motion is more important than range. The lunge, while performed in one time, can be broken down into six phases – three to deliver the attack and three to recover from it. All of these phases are to be performed consecutively and not concurrently.

The first three phases of the long under hand thrust deliver the lunge. First, the arm is extended. Next, just before the shoulder joint rises, as the arm reaches full extension, the torso is leaned forward. Then, the foot is moved forward and bending the leading knee moves the weight of the body forward. This should move the sword along a long straight course to aid in penetrating the enemy's body along with the extraction of the sword afterwards.

The three phases of the long under hand thrust recovery

The final three phases returns the fencer to a proper guard. First, as if

being pulled from the back of the skull, the fencer begins the extraction of the torso. Beginning this motion with the head is important, as it will easily bring the fencer back into the appropriate stance with the weight supported by the back leg. It is also significant in keeping the fencers sword extended in front of them. To not begin the recovery with the head means the elbow will be thrown backwards in the action of the fencer transferring their weight backward, resulting in the elbow moving too far backwards and making it impossible to maintain a proper guard. Next, after the torso has been recovered, the leading knee is straightened and the back knee bent to take the weight of the body; this should also recover the leading foot to its original place. Finally, the sword returns to its proper guard.

Inside extended lunge   Outside extended lunge

There are some additional subtleties and mechanics to Giganti's long under hand thrust that are worth noting. Each phase serves a significant function in conducting a safe attack. First, the arm is not meant to deliver the force of the attack – the arm creates a solid foundation so that the movement of the feet and the body can deliver the attack. It is important to ensure that, while extending the arm, neither the sword nor the shoulder joint rise, nor should the elbow fully extend and lock. These errors will compromise the subsequent phases of the long under hand thrust. Another consideration is the placement of the front foot, which should be to the inside or outside, but never in the centre. This means that the long under hand thrust will be delivered on an angle to the opponent and never directly toward them. With the arm solidly in guard, the leading foot will advance

along the line described by the fencer's heels (anywhere from 15 to 30 degrees away from the line of engagement). With the solid structure created by the arm, the weight of the body is transferred forward down the line described by the fencer's heels. This serves to either push the enemy's sword out of engagement. The extension of the torso adds additional force and distance to this action, as well as lowering the fencer's profile, providing less of a target for the opponent.

When practicing the Long under hand thrust against an opponent, a common problem is the blade sliding along the opponents mask, or not taking a strong line for the opponent's face. This typically is caused by the fencer not taking the time to ensure that the structure of the arm is firm; as a result, the fencer is likely leaning the torso and stepping too soon.

Lesson 4: Why We Commence with the Single Sword

In my first book of arms I intend to deal with only two sorts of weapons, that is: the single Sword & Sword and dagger. I reserve the treatment of others to those whom merely to please men, try bringing light at first to all sorts of weapons. Because the Sword is the most common & usual weapon of all the others, I want you to start with it. After you know the play of the single Sword well, you shall also know in some small part of the management of all sorts of arms. But, it follows in all parts of the world, you will not always have use to carry the dagger, target, or round buckler & often frays occur with combat of single Sword. I exhort all learn first the play of the single Sword, which will be present in all disputes with the dagger, target, or the round buckler. It also follows, that it often occurs that the dagger, target, or round buckler falls from the hand. It is possible for a man to defend & wound the enemy with the single Sword. Only after you exercise the play of single Sword, knowing well it's wardings & woundings, then you shall have Sword & dagger.

Giganti clearly states the reason for the ordering of his work, with fencing with the single sword coming before sword and dagger. Giganti mentions the use of a small shield, either square (the target) or round (the round buckler), but he does not cover the use of these defensive weapons in this work – Giganti briefly describes the use of these defensive weapons in his

Libro Secondo.... *What is implied in Giganti's rationale is that the techniques of the single sword form the basis for all combat with the sword, regardless of whether a second weapon is used or not. This will be significant in Giganti's depiction of fencing with the sword and dagger as his discussion moves from specific plays and techniques to an abstract discussion of tactics and options.*

Lesson 5: Guards, or Postures

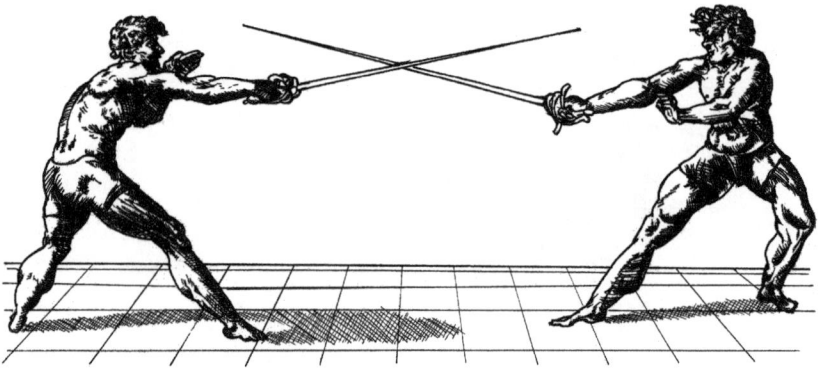

Plate 2

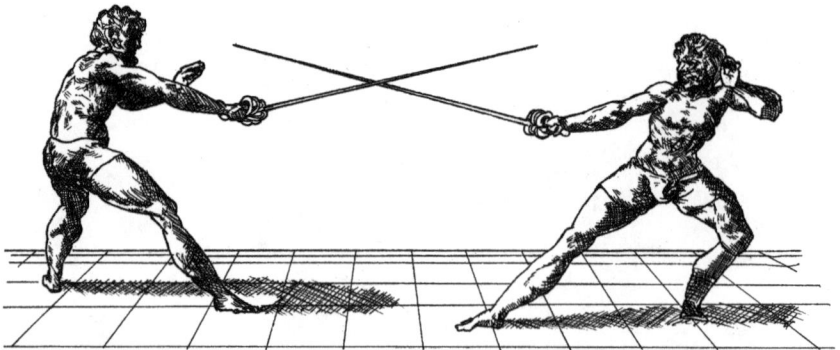

Plate 3

Many are the guards of the single Sword & thus many are the counterguards. In my first Book I am not be able to teach them all, only two sorts of guards & counterguards. These will be able to serve you for all the lessons in the pictures of this Book. First, you must bear many things in mind when you come to do this. You must go to bind the enemy outside the measure safe from his Sword by setting yours upon his. In this way it is impossible for him to wound you without using two times, one in the circling of the Sword & the other the wounding. In this way you accommodate yourself against all guards, high or low. It follows that you may easily see; never giving a commodious strike & occasion to your enemy, making it impossible for you to be wounded in a single time. This is done by taking care that his point shall not be towards the middle of your torso. To this end you are to spring with nimbleness & strength, upon his sword. Thus, it is impossible for you to be wounded.

You cover then the enemy's Sword with that of yours as you can see in this picture. Thus, the enemy's Sword shall be outside of your torso & impossible for him to wound you without circling his Sword. Accommodating yourself with the feet strong, torso firm, the sword arm extended & strong for warding & wounding, as is shown in the pictures. When you see the enemy in a high or low guard & you do not set the counter to that guard, you are not safe from the enemy's Sword; you shall be in danger. This is good then when you see your enemy has little science & less practice than you. Since you could be in danger of crossing and both wounding each other, or he can set you warding obediently: with a feint, circling his sword, or other ways that he can interfere with you. However, if you will shelter yourself from the enemy's sword, as I warned you of before, he cannot move or to do anything without you being aware of it and without you having the opportunity of warding yourself. In these pictures which are here you see two guards with the sword forward & two counterguards for covering the Sword. One binds the enemy on the inside & the other goes on the outside, as these pictures show you.* As I will go on to show in the next lessons.

---

* In plates 2 and 3 what is shown is as follows. Outside guard (plate 2 right figure), Inside counterguard (plate 2 left figure), inside guard (plate 3 right figure), outside counterguard (plate 3 left figure).

There are only two guards in Giganti's system of fencing with the single sword, although he does acknowledge that there are a myriad of guards that exist outside the confines of this work. These guards are those of the inside and outside. Giganti makes a further distinction between guards and counterguards. In practice there is no difference between the guard and the counterguard; it is, rather, a distinction between which of the two swords is closer to the line of engagement and thus controlling the fight. One fencer sets in a guard and the other then counters that guard with the opposite guard. For example, an outside guard is countered by an inside counterguard and an inside guard in countered by an outside counterguard. As Giganti observes, counterguards are meant to prevent the opponent from making an attack in a single time. By forcing their blade away from the centre of the fight, the opponent is forced to make a preceding action before throwing an under hand thrust. Given Giganti's admonishment in Lesson 2 about attacking when the opponent is not making an attack, this action preceding the opponent's under hand thrust is the ideal time for the fencer to throw an under hand thrust of their own.

Once again, there are important mechanical points to observe in practice. Both of these guards are to be held low, with the forearm near parallel to the ground roughly at the base of the ribcage. It may take time for the student to find the perfect position, but in the end it will be one in which the sword is held easily and the arm is not worn out by the position. If the upper arm is sore from holding the sword, it is likely that the guards are being held too low. Giganti emphasized the importance of holding the arm at this level by noting this guard will be effective 'against all guards, high, or low.' *The reason for not raising the guard higher is discussed in the third lesson on the long under hand thrust – by raising the arm the shoulder joint will move out of alignment with the socket, hindering the structure required for the long under hand thrust and the guards.*

It is important when setting in these guards to hold the opponent's sword well away from the centre of the body; the off-line placement of the leading foot will accomplish some of this task. The illustrations make it clear that the leading foot is moved toward the side that the fencer's guard or counterguard is set. This positioning of the feet permits the fencer's body to be used in pushing the opponent's sword off line, or to permit the fencer to slip away from the opponent's sword.

The placement of the feet is of critical importance in understanding Giganti's system of the fence. When interpreting the following lessons it is important to understand where the feet are supposed to be. When the fencers have established the guard and counterguard at the beginning of a play, the feet will remain in the position defined by this initial guard-counterguard relationship throughout the subsequent actions. The only exception to this rule is when the fencer is specifically instructed to retire out of measure where it is safe to change guards. This positioning of the feet will define whether the fencer is to bind and affront the opponent's sword or whether they will slip away from it when the delivering the point.

Lesson 6: Declaration of Wounding in Time

Plate 4

This picture teaches you to wound your enemy in the time when he circles his Sword. You shall do this by going to bind the enemy outside of measure, placing your sword upon his on your inside path. As you will see the picture of the first guard, so that he will not be able to wound you without circling the Sword. Then you in that same time as he is circling to wound, thrust your Sword forward twisting the wrist in the same time, then you wound to the face, as you see in the picture. If you intend to ward & then to wound, it will not succeed; as the enemy has time to ward. You shall endanger yourself. But, if you in the time when he is circling his Sword, quickly enter forward with yours twisting the wrist, thus warding, the enemy will have difficulty in being able to ward you. Having done this &

wounding thus, you shall not be by the enemy. For your safety return backwards outside of measure with your Sword upon the enemy's, never abandoning it.

In case the enemy does not circle his Sword to wound, you should go to bind outside the measure & quickly throw the point where he is uncovered, returning back outside the measure leaning your sword upon his.

This lesson describes the first play of the manual. This play is the articulation of the concepts discussed in Giganti's lesson on the Time and Measure. This is the basic action of a fencer warding the opponent's sword in the same time as they throw the long under hand thrust. This is done by simply turning the sword from one counterguard to the other.

This play begins with the opponent in an outside guard and the fencer binds him with an inside counterguard. This means that the leading foot of each combatant is to the fencer's inside. The opponent circles the fencer's sword in the first time – having been prevented from attacking in one time by the fencer's counterguard – and then in the second time the opponent intends to take an outside counterguard and launch a long under hand thrust. In the first time, at the beginning of the opponent's circling, the fencer turns their wrist into the outside guard, this catches the opponent's sword mid-circle; the fencer throws the long under hand thrust in the same time as the twisting of the wrist. Given the orientation of the fencer having the sword to the outside and the foot to the inside the movement of the under hand thrust will carry the fencer to the inside and away from the opponent's sword. Because the opponent is throwing the blow with full intention, the fencer must be mindful to extend the sword arm, and only throwing the torso and leg if the blow falls short of the opponent. To move the torso and legs too soon will result in the measure between the two closing to quickly for the fencer's sword to attack with the point.

Lesson 44 suggests a possible response to warding in which opponent could dispatch the fencer. If the opponent is quick enough, they can shift their weight backward while leaving the arm extended and in guard. This action will bring the opponent's forte *across the fencer's* debole, *with this new blade relationship the opponent can re-exert their bind, return their weight forward, and, throw point in the same line as their previous attack.*

Lesson 7: The True Way of Going to Bind the Enemy and Strike while he Circles his Sword

Plate 5

You must learn from this picture that when your enemy is in guard with the sword to his left, high or low, you must go to bind his sword to your outside, outside the measure, with your Sword upon his, at pains to touch his, with a proper and strong step. With your Sword in action of warding & wounding with the eye lively as you saw in the second Picture of the guards & counterguards.[*] Standing in this way recommended to you, your enemy will not be able to wound with the point without circling his Sword. While he is circling, twist your wrist & in that same time throw the under hand thrust as you are taught in the fourth picture.[†] Having thrown

---

[*] Lesson four.
[†] Lesson six.

this under hand thrust, quickly and in one time return backwards outside of measure more to your right and resting your sword upon his. The reason being, he will want to circle anew, in which case, you are to throw the same under hand thrust twisting the wrist, as above retiring outside of measure. For each time he circles, every other time to use this twist of the wrist & throw this under hand thrust. For you to do this play well, it behoves you to exercise it often, from this is learned the knowledge of binding & wounding with extension & great nimbleness. I warn you, always stand with the torso firm & binding strongly with the forte of your Sword. If your enemy throws at you strongly, you bind with your forte, then, he will lay disordered & you may wound where he is uncovered. This, must be the first lesson to be learned of single Sword. From this first one all the others that I have put in this book are born. Knowing how to do this in time you learn the warding of all the cuts & resolute points which come for the head, as I will teach that these things go hand in hand with the subsequent lessons.

This play is identical to the previous one, except it begins with the opposite guard-counterguard relationship. The opponent holds an inside guard and the fencer gains the opponent's blade with an outside counterguard. When the opponent circles his sword in the first time, the fencer extends their arm and turns their wrist into the inside guard, the under hand thrust carries the fencer away from the enemy's sword.

Giganti uses the second half of this lesson to provide additional information to the reader. The first piece of information is that this technique of twisting the wrist – or warding – is fundamental to his system of fencing. If the opponent circles the sword to ward and throw the under hand thrust in the same time is the simplest response. Giganti suggests that practicing this play frequently will improve binding, in particular the proper balance of the torso and using the forte *to dominate the opponent's blade. These are indeed important aspects to the proper execution of binding in the under hand thrust. Giganti concludes by stating that practice will breed the knowledge of theory, and that in practice it is more important to understand objectives than the precise elements of theory.*

Lesson 8: The True Way of Circling the Sword

In these two pictures* I have put here above, we have taught you to wound the enemy while he circles his Sword. And because this did not lie in my lesson, it shall no longer be strange. I will show the knowledge of how to circle the Sword. Therefore note, that your enemy being accommodated by being in any strong guard, in the instance that he will move to bind and throw where you are uncovered. If he knows as much as you, he shall always do so with the Swords in contact. But, I want you, with a nimble wrist to circle your Sword below the furnishing enemy's and throw the point in the same time where he lays uncovered. This is the true & safe way of knowing how to circle the Sword & wound in one time. Which if you shall circle your sword without turning the wrist, it shall give time & place to your enemy to wound you. You will see this proved very well in practice. If your enemy will ward, you must seek to circle in the above said way, always turning the wrist, &, as often as he wards, circle always in the way above, this is most secure. Then throwing the under hand thrust in the same time as you circle. This way of circling it is no less necessary as that, which was taught in the declaration of the previous noted pictures on the way of knowing how to ward; after those this is the principle thing, which you should seek to know in managing the single Sword. Thus I exhort unto you to practice these two things well, when being in measure against the enemy,

---

* Lessons six and seven.

how in time of circling the Sword, knowing how to circle nimbly & well & in the time of warding, to know how to ward equally well.

Giganti introduces the proper technique for circling the sword in this lesson. Giganti's circling of the sword is meant to break the opponent's counterguard and move his sword away from the center of the fight. This explains Giganti's preference for twisting the wrist, as it imparts more momentum to the fencer's blade and applies a sharp beat as the fencer takes the counterguard from their opponent. This beat also provides a moment in which the long under hand thrust can be thrown, but only if the circling and the throw overlap as Giganti advises.

To circle the sword, the fencer's hand quickly moves to the opposite guard and then back to the original guard. The blade, in particular the tip, of the sword is not to be forced through this action; instead, the blade is pulled along by the motion of the hand. The movement of the hand into the opposite guard will begin the blade's movement away from the enemy's sword and then gravity will begin the downward motion of the sword below the guard, or "furnishing," of the opponent's sword. The momentum of the sword and the return of the hand to the original guard will pull the sword into the counterguard. The second aspect of Giganti's circling of the sword is that it should always be conducted with an extension of the arm in the same time, and the lunge completed immediately afterwards.

Lesson 9: The Counter Circle Inside of the Sword

Plate 6

In this picture I present & show you another way of warding & wounding by the way of the counter circle. It is done in the following way. Having covered your enemy's Sword, if he wants to wound you it behoves him, to circle. While he circles, I want you to circle yourself, so that your Sword returns to its first place, covering that enemy's. But, the circle being done, splitting the time, throw the under hand thrust where he is uncovered, wanting your torso somewhat towards his right side. Holding the arm extended forward, when he comes thence to wound you, there you are able to wound. Having thrown the under hand thrust, you must return backwards outside of measure.

The counter circle is very good in demonstrating Giganti's concept of time in fencing. The proper moment of the fencer's attack will be made clear through practice, reinforcing Giganti's system of teaching through the repetition observed in lesson 7. With practice, the fencer will develop an instinctive rhythm of throwing the under hand thrust in the pause between the opponent's attack and recovery. This instinctive moment is that of 'splitting the time,' which some contemporary Italian masters called "contratempo." *This means the attack strikes the opponent between two of the opponent's motions, or times. In this case, the strike comes between the opponent's attack and recovery.*[*]

This play begins much like that of lesson seven, with the fencer in an outside counterguard against their opponent's inside guard. When the opponent circles the fencer's sword, in order to throw the long under hand thrust, the fencer follows the opponent's sword by circling. The result is that the swords return to the original orientation, but now the opponent is extended forward with the under hand thrust and thus disordered. The fencer then throws their point.

For this and the coming plays it is important to pay attention to the individual steps of the long under hand thrust. Of particular importance is in ensuring that the arm has been extended fully before stepping and throwing the weight forward. If you notice that the blade is not firmly hitting the opponent (i.e. slapping or sliding along their mask) this is an indicator that the arm is not being fully extended before the other parts of the attack are being executed. It is also important to note that depending on the speed of 'splitting the time' the fencer's offensive action often requires little else but the extension of the arm. The remaining phases of the long underhand thrust can be used if the opponent has begun their recovery out of the failed attack.

---

[*] One of my students, Wayne, has the jarring habit of throwing the under hand thrust before the pause – this technique works just as well, although it is somewhat discombobulating to be on the receiving end of it.

Lesson 10: The Counter Circle Outside of the Sword

Plate 7

This way of wounding is by way of counter circling to the outside, it is similar to the counter circle of the inside, only the placement is different. When your enemy is standing in guard & you come to bind, you must place yourself against his guard when you are outside of measure, safely with your Sword to his outside, making your enemy be resolute in his circling. While he is circling, you circle in that same time, turning the point of your Sword underneath his with the wrist, go to his blade resting with forte of the blade of your sword, carrying the arm long & extended, straightening the torso & lengthening the step, as is seen in the picture. Thus you come to wound him, which he cannot heed. But, in your circle take heed yourself, that the enemy having thrown his Sword strongly, you do not want to bend the enemy's Sword & he wounds you. It behoves you when circling, to carry your torso backwards, so that it will lay in safety. You may assume when enemy has thrown strongly, he will be disconcerted & you will then stand in a better position to wound & he will come to be wounded on your sword, where you will. Heeding always of holding your sword outside of your torso,* so that you shall not be wounded.

This play begins in the same manner as lesson six, with the fencer in an inside counterguard to the opponent's outside guard. While this attack is similar to the previous counter circle, the fencer must make sure that the counter circle and the extension to attack does not overlap. Giganti notes this by writing "when circling, to carry your torso backwards, so that it will lay in safety." In essence, Giganti is saying that the fencer should wait until the last possible moment within a time to conduct the action. This is good advice for all of Giganti's system of fencing, but of critical importance here. Giganti completes the lesson by admonishing the reader to hold their sword—and the opponent's sword—away from the centre line to the inside or the outside.

---

* This does not refer to a guard on the outside, rather it is a reminder for the fencer to hold the opponent's tip far from the body.

Lesson 11: Declaration of the Feint Shown with Circling the Sword with the Wrist

Plate 8

Varied are the manners of wounding & as a consequence varied shall be my lessons. But, this should not surprise you, should I recount all things to you that one must be able to do in this profession. These being infinite, my work would be over long & bring the reader to boredom. Therefore, I shall go forth to those things that appear to me to be more beautiful, artificial, & useful, which are born from other things more simple & of less artifice.

Amongst all the ways of wounding by artifice, the feint, in my opinion, exceeds all others. This is nothing else than pretending to do one thing & then doing another. It is done in diverse ways & they are these. I want you, to set yourself on your feet & on the inside, with your Sword in front, the right arm extended to give your enemy opportunity to come to bind. Be wary, as he comes thence in measure with you, whether he wants to wound you with his feet firm or if he wants to step to the right past you. He knows you are to circle. When you do this with the Sword; circle the Sword with the wrist & bind with your edge a point to his face. But, throw the enemy's Sword wide. If he does not intend to seek yours; if the enemy does not ward, you must throw resolutely, then you shall wound. But, if he wards, in his warding you re-circle the Sword & wound him as you see in this picture, because in this way, the enemy without being aware of it, is throwing himself at you to be wounded. But, take care when re-circling you do not let him catch your Sword, for which you will prove empty in your thought. In circling, carry the head and torso back somewhat so you see the business of your enemy. For if he is throwing & you do not withdraw backwards when making the encounter, you both could be wounded. Of more help is to take care that you go with the true edge of your sword to the blade enemy's Sword, wanting your pulse upward in the wounding so your Sword is upon the enemy's *debole*. Giving the under hand thrust, either resolutely or feint, you return quickly back outside of measure. If the feint is done in this manner it is safe. First showing the sword to the enemy's face or chest. Lengthening the arm without making a step. If the enemy goes to ward you, you in the same time circle your Sword & accompany it forward with the step, in this way you will wound him by surprise. But, if he does not ward, increase the step & strike. This it is the way of the feint.

Albeit, the two following pictures appear similar; however, there are differences between them, because they have different ways of binding, even though they are almost identical ways for wounding. Even if it would have been enough to have presented you by one single picture with which we could discuss & teach you different ways of binding to wound. Instead, I decided to insert two that are very different between themselves in order to bring evidence for these diverse ways of binding; which I will demonstrate to you in their declarations.

Giganti's feint builds on the concepts laid down by the counter circle techniques of lessons 9 and 10. However, in the feint Giganti introduces plays beginning with the opponent holding the inside counterguard against the fencer's outside guard. In this play, the fencer over extends their sword in the outside guard in order to encourage the opponent to attempt to bind and attack. When the opponent attacks, the fencer conducts and large defensive circling with the sword placing their forte *on their opponent's* debole. *This clears the opponent's incoming blow wide from the body. Like the counter circle, the fencer splits the time after the opponent's offensive momentum is spent. Once the opponent pauses between the times, the fencer* launches the long under hand thrust for the opponent's face. This must be done with the full intention of hitting the opponent with this under hand thrust, if the fencer succeeds, so much the better. Only when the tip is a very short distance from the opponent's face will the opponent execute the instinctive sweeping flinch response on which the feint relies.

The opponent's action at this point in the play requires some explanation. This forms the basis of additional plays that are worthwhile to practice, as they form a workable counter to lessons 8 and 9. Giganti does mention this action, but not until much later in the work – lesson 44. When faced with the fencer's final under hand thrust in lessons 8 and 9, the opponent, if not over extended, can return their weight backwards, keeping the sword extended. In the same time the opponent wards into the opposite guard. This action brings the opponent's forte over the fencer's debole and gives the opponent the counterguard. Having gained this position the opponent can then shift their weight forward again and throw another long under hand thrust. Of course, if the opponent can easily execute this counter, it is typically an indicator that the opponent was not sufficiently resolute in their initial attack. This should serve as a warning to fencers that they should only respond offensively to resolute attacks, and that in practicing Giganti's plays both fencers need to actively attempt to hit each other (fence with intention) both in drills and sparring.

Returning to the action of the feint: when the fencer's tip has come close to the opponent's face, the opponent will often instinctively attempt to draw the weight backward and turn the hand over in order to defend against the incoming attack (in the manner described in the previous paragraph). The fencer is to take the motion of their opponent's warding to begin their circle under the opponent's sword and finish throwing the under hand thrust in the same time.

Lesson 12: The Way of Wounding in the Body with Single Sword when You Are in Measure with the Swords in Contact

Plate 9

In the present picture is an artificial manner of wounding the enemy in the body and securing his Sword, which makes it impossible for him to offend while you step by him to wound him. It is to be done in this manner. It behoves you to set in a guard with the Sword in front to the left side. If the enemy comes thence binding you & covering your Sword with his; let him come until he finds himself in measure with you. As he is in measure; you circle, placing your Sword inside of his directing your point against your enemy's face. If he does not go warding you, you wound him resolutely, going as I said by turning the pulse to raise your true edge to his and carrying your body somewhat across. But, while you circle, if the enemy comes thence to bind & wound you, do not throw the point. But, you must hold it somewhat to your outside & in the same time as he wants to ward & wound, you re-circle Sword below the furnishing of his. That done, aim for the enemy's body, thus you strike him in the body safely, increasing with the Sword somewhat, as you see in the picture. It helps if the circle & re-circle are in the same time, never holding firm to it, so that the enemy cannot find it. When he shows he is going to parry, you are to passage outside his torso towards his back, taking care to place your hand upon his hilt. That effect of the passage makes it impossible for him to wound you, but, it enables you to wound him in any which manner and place you like & please.

In this play the fencer assumes an inside guard with the arm overextended to encourage the opponent to bind and attack in the outside counterguard. When the opponent attacks, the fencer conducts a wide circle of their sword, similar in character to the one discussed in the previous play and the counter-circles. Once the opponent's attack has been gathered up and set aside wide to the fencer's inside, the tip is dropped and the hand raised so that the sword is in line to attack in the inside counterguard. The fencer attacks the opponent's face resolutely – if they hit, so much the better. If the opponent attempts to defend themselves by warding (upward and to their inside), the fencer is to circle again and then passage forward with the inside foot, seize the opponent's hilt, and deliver the point of the sword.

Lesson 13: Your Passage with the Feint in Distance

Plate 10

This is an artificial manner of passaging behind the enemy, so that he is not safe. The effect that is shown, as you see in the present picture, where you step with a feint going to wound the enemy, is of great consideration. It is done in this way. It behoves you to see in which guard your enemy is placed. If it is opportune, you go to bind him in guard directing the point of your sword against his face. As you find yourself almost in measure, if you see he is standing waiting & not moving, throw your point against the face, as is shown in lesson 10. If he does not ward strongly, do the effect of the lesson 11. As you would do in other feints. But, if he wards, with the Swords in contact do both of the following. Quickly return backwards outside of measure & set in the same guard as you held first. As you are almost in measure, feign a throw to his face with the same point. While he is going to ward, circle the wrist below the enemy's hilt with the point of your Sword, taking care to hold the enemy's Sword outside of your torso. Then in the same time passage, going with your Sword upon the furnishing of his accompanied by the left hand. Quickly setting it upon the enemy's hilt, so that he cannot strike a back hand blow in your face. In this way, without a doubt you will wound him, without him being aware of it. Having done this, leap outside of measure & recovering the Sword from your enemy, securely in the way of above, lower your sword returning to wound him with two or three resolute & irrepressible points.

In order to match the picture, this play starts with the fencer in an outside counterguard covering the opponent's inside guard. The fencer then throws at the opponent's face, striking resolutely if the opponent fails to ward. If the opponent wards, the fencer circles under the opponent's sword recovering backwards and then makes a feigned thrust at the opponent's face in the outside guard. Giganti then assumes the opponent will ward this second throw. The fencer re-circles their sword and passages grasping the opponent's hilt with the inside hand and throws the point through the opponent's body. Although Giganti does not mention it, it is possible that the opponent could fail to ward the second blow; in which case the fencer should ward to the inside guard and deliver the point resolutely. The primary difficulty of practicing this play is that it relies heavily on the instinctive flinch, and unless each attack is delivered with proper intention and intensity the play will be difficult to practice.

Lesson 14: The Passage with the Feint Raising the Point of the Sword

Plate 43

This is another sort of circle & feint which is not often used, which is similar to the two preceding pictures & is done thus. It behoves you to stand in guard with the Sword to the left side, with the arm extended & long. Letting the enemy to come to bind in the way described. As he is in measure, circle your Sword raising the point of his. If you see that he is not warding, you throw at him strongly & resolutely, as I have told you, you will not need to apply any other feint. But, if he wards, you are not to be firm with your Sword, but, to escape the guard furnished by the enemy's Sword. Passaging in the way above. Then you wound him in the body. You then return as is said above.

This play has the fencer holding an over extended inside guard to which the opponent comes to bind and attack with an outside counterguard. Against this attack, the fencer circles the opponent's sword and then raises their sword to throw an over hand thrust in the inside line, while at the same time raising the point of the opponent's sword out of an offensive line with the forward and upward motion of the hilt. As with the other feints, if the opponent does not respond by warding to the inside, the attack is resolutely driven home. This is the action portrayed in the picture above. However, if the opponent wards to the inside and upward in an attempt to defend, the fencer circles again, passages with the left foot, and seizes the opponent's hilt with the left hand as seen in lessons 12 and 13.

This lesson has been illustrated to assist in explaining the interpretation of the play, however, the illustration does not portray the end of the play. Like the illustration for the next lesson this illustrates the result of the opponent not warding the attack that raises the point of their sword.

Lesson 15: The Feint in Distance to the Face

Plate 11

This Feint is not different from the other, if not only in that the first one is characterized by the circling below the hilt of the Sword, and this one it is characterized by a rising to throw at the face enemy's, this under hand thrust if he wards, you feint, and if he does not ward you go resolutely. In the pause you observe the same guards, distances, & measures; and parry carrying the torso, and the Sword, as is seen in the picture, and quickly having thrown the point it is necessary you return outside of measure; Of the utmost importance is to know how to feint naturally, thus it cannot be distinguished from the resolute. Which is done in this manner. You must circle the point (as it shall be the same for all examples) rising to the outside of the face, and when you step towards him, with your point underneath the enemy's hilt you go to wound to the inside; it behoves you to make the point with the circle wound to the face or body. And it is intended that this Feint be very natural: but heed never to make an ill feint, if the enemy does not go to parry you resolutely, you would be in danger of wounding you both, & you will lay in peril.

This lesson and plate can easily confuse the reader. This picture is not used in the same way as the other illustrations in Giganti's work, which show the final time of the play. Rather, this picture demonstrates the possible wound delivered in the middle of the play.

Both the fencer and the opponent start in an outside guard, the fencer circles their sword under the opponent's, the fencer then affronts the opponent's sword with an outside counterguard. The force of this bind is increased by passage the left foot forward and reaching the inside hand to grasp the opponent's hilt. If the opponent fails to apply a sufficient defensive response by moving their sword strongly upward and to their outside, the attack is applied as is demonstrated in the picture. If the opponent does ward to the outside and upwards with force, the fencer circles and gives the under hand thrust.

Lesson 16: The True Way to Give a Point with the Single Sword while the Enemy is Throwing a Cut

Plate 12

This picture teaches you to use the time to give an under hand thrust to your enemy's face, when he throws a high cut to your head. It is while he is raising his Sword that you are able to give him the under hand thrust, while his Sword is in the air. You shall arrive first. How this is done, take note. It shall be sent from whatever guard you please, you going to bind your enemy. As you are in measure, if your enemy throws a cut at your head, in the raising of his Sword, you take advantage of that time. Enter forward & throw your Sword at his face, which without a doubt you will wound him, while the enemy's Sword is in the air as seen in the picture. But, in so doing turn the pulse in and up & the true edge of your Sword upward, having extended the arm long & high. You make the guard of your sword cover your head, so that the enemy in the descent of his Sword, shall find you covered & make it impossible for him to offend you. It is good therefore to throw your point nimbly; which if it is not nimble, the enemy might be able to parry & wound you. After you have thrown, nimbly return backwards outside of measure, securing your Sword against that of your enemy.

I do not desire to set down in this First Book all the ways of warding the cut, for there are many. But, I put only this one before you. This appears to me to be of much utility & the most commodious for knowing to recognize the time & to be of service, which is necessary to know in such an occasion.

Giganti does not describe cutting in Scola overò Teatro*..., saving detailed discussion of the subject for* Libro Secondo.... *However, Giganti's system of cutting is summarized in the glossary in the front matter. This lesson illustrates the basis of the defence against cuts. The concepts discussed in this lesson are used to defend against any cut. The timing of the defence is simple; the fencer delivers the under hand thrust to the opponent's face as the opponent draws back the sword to develop the momentum for the cut. Giganti also instructs the fencer to turn the true edge toward the direction of the cut; this instruction is an extra safeguard for the fencer should the under hand thrust fail to stop the motion of the cut.*

Lesson 17: The True Way of Wounding Safely with Single Sword with Both Hands

Plate 13

This picture shows you a way of safely wounding the enemy; which is impossible for him to ward. It is done in two manners.

First, it behoves you to find the occasion to be in contact with the enemy's Sword & to have his outside of yours. Then, you affront with your Sword against your enemy's face, which, if he does not ward strongly you strike him in the face, as you have seen in these four pictures. But, if he wards well & strong, you increase with a step of the left foot placing your left hand upon your Sword. Thrust hard with both hands, directing your point against the enemy's body, furnishing your Sword low, as is seen in the present picture. Take care to do all these things in one time.

It follows easily then, that should you be in a guard of the aforesaid manner; but, with his Sword inside of yours. I want you to circle your

Sword in action of wounding to his outside. In the same time that you circle your Sword, place your left hand upon your Sword & with the force of both hands beat your enemy's Sword with yours, when it is beaten far off quickly passage with the left foot forward, as you see in the picture. But, for this to succeed well, it is best you take care to do all of this in one time, that is to say circle the Sword, place the hand, beat the enemy's Sword, & passage forward with the left foot. Should all of these things not be done in one time, in that case you will not succeed & you shall be in peril. You shall want to do this like some valiant man whom knows how to circle nimbly & well with his Sword. Therefore, for you to succeed in this, you must to do all nimbly & improvise.

The first play begins with the fencer holding the outside counterguard against the opponent's inside guard. The fencer extends the arm to attack the opponent's face. If the opponent fails to ward, the under hand thrust is delivered. If the opponent attempts to ward the incoming attack the fencer passages forward with the inside foot and in the same time places their inside hand on mid-blade of the fencer's sword. The fencer then pushes the opponent's downward and throws the under hand thrust maintaining the inside counterguard.

The second play begins with the opponent in the inside counterguard covering the fencer's outside guard. In the same time the fencer passages and places their inside hand on mid-blade of the fencer's sword. The fencer then pushes the opponent's sword downward and throws the under hand thrust maintaining the inside counterguard.

Lesson 18: The True Way of Parrying the Cut or Back Hand Blow, which Comes for the Leg

Plate 14

In this lesson, which explains the fore hand or back hand cut to the leg. I cannot say anything if I do not teach that it is possible to parry and wound the enemy in the same time. Here is the contrary, I say the enemy lies to be attacked before that time in a straight line from the point of the Sword. This is necessary when the enemy's fore hand or back hand blow descends for the leg. It is required, when he is lengthening his step and body and carrying his face forward. While the enemy is descending to wound you, then take your forward leg away backwards. He, being unable to ward, wounds himself, but, he is not able then to wound you afterwards, as well. You then, (as other times I have said) return backwards outside of measure.

And the present lesson is very artificial. Thus it is a technique wanted by the trade, for to be able to do it will be of service to you in such an occasion, as the Picture shows you clearly.

This technique is a universal one in fencing manuals throughout history. If the opponent throws a cut for the fencers outside leg from either direction, the fencer responds with a reunite and throwing an under or over hand thrust at the opponent's face. The passage of the outside leg backwards also plays an important role in Giganti's sword and dagger techniques. In a sporting context this technique can also work against a thrust against the leading leg. However, in actual combat to do so would have been a risky proposition; the fencer's sword could pass through the opponent's head, thus momentum permitting the opponent to close distance to hit the fencer's leg.

Lesson 19: Of the Inquartata or Slip of the Torso

Plate 15

It is Necessary for the *Inquartata* or slipping for you to be able to control your body. But, this ordinarily is not used in the Schools, it is only the French who exercise the torso. In truth, many are these Slips or *Inquartatas*, but, I have chosen to show only the three I judge the best. Which, appear in the present picture, in my mind are the most secure and beautiful.

The first of these has you set in guard outside of measure with your right foot extended forward and inside, standing strongly to your right flank, with the Sword arm long, extended, & holding the point to the enemy's Sword. You permit the enemy to go to bind you, as he comes almost in measure, you must circle your Sword in a feint a little wide. In the time when your enemy should parry, you must re-circle it, turning it to the way you held first, going with the circle to the blade of his Sword, in this manner. You did not have to circle very quickly, in order to wound the enemy. When you desire to circle your Sword, and go to wound you should be in peril, it follows it should be done in two times. Carry the left leg across, and likewise the left shoulder. You then turn to do the effect (as it is seen in the picture), whereupon a point, either to the face or body, in a way that he will not even be aware of it. Hold the arm firm, with the hilt of your Sword covering you, holding off the enemy's Sword, holding yours to the eye of his face. Take care not to turn your face with your torso, as one would normally do, for you will then find yourself in peril, and not see your business. Having turned your back with your Sword you return outside of measure immediately, safely as above.

This play begins with the fencer holding an extended outside counterguard to entice the opponent into circling, binding, and attacking with the inside counterguard. The fencer meets this attack with a wide defensive circle, and then throws an outside under hand thrust at the opponent's face as in other feints. Of course, if the opponent fails to make a defensive response the under hand thrust is delivered to the face. If the opponent twists the wrist to their outside, the fencer circles the sword again and holds themselves in a vulnerable outside guard. The opponent then throws in an inside counterguard. Then, wards into an inside counterguard, and, in the same time, steps with the inside foot in a circular fashion outside and in front of the fencer's outside foot.

Giganti gives some important general advice in this lesson on the inquartata, *which is significant to his entire system of fencing and doubly so for delivering the* inquartata. *This is hinted at by Giganti's admonishment to the fencer to* "turn… it [the sword] to the way you held it first," *which instructs the fencer to hold for a time before moving their foot and body into the action of the* inquartata. *This pause gives the illusion to the opponent of an opening permitting them to commit fully to an attack. The circular motion of the back leg considerably shortens the range of the fencer's attack. As a result, the fencer must rely, in part, on the forward motion of the opponent to run on to the end of the fencer's sword. In order to ensure this, the fencer must hold their actions until the last possible moment in each time. This gives the opponent a larger period of time to consider and commit to an attack. In general, waiting until the last possible moment in all actions will assist in giving the opponent more impetus to fully commit to attacks while also giving them less time to respond to the fencer's actions. This also speaks to the importance of remaining calm and using a slower cadence and wide measure in sparring, giving the opponent a greater sense of security and a willingness to fully commit to offensive actions.*

Lesson 20: On the Inquartata, or Slip of the Torso

This other *Inquartata* is similar from the first, except in the manner of wounding. That is to say, to have care in going with your blade for the enemy's Sword, to wound him below his pommel. As it is seen in the picture, by raising your arm with the wrist. Turning yourself to wound, do not turn your back to the enemy and do not come forward to the press, which you should go in peril. Instead, you will be able to return safely outside of measure. This *Inquartata* is very difficult to ward, I say near impossible, when it is done with judgement.

This is a slight variation on the previous play; the blade action is identical to the previous lesson. The differences lie in how the fencer moves their body and sword. The sword hilt is raised and the wound is delivered below the enemy's pommel. Also, in this inquartata, *instead of the circular step with the back foot, the fencer turns their inside foot directly backwards on the ball of the foot and leans to the outside. The motion is very similar to the* scanso, *or twist of the Torso found in Capoferro.*[*]

---

[*] Capoferro, plate 17.

Lesson 21: The Third Inquartata or Slip of the Torso

This third *Inquartata* is the best, and safest of all, if it is done in this manner. Set in your Guard, as in the other two, holding the Sword on your right flank with the arm extended and firm. As the enemy comes thence to bind you with his Sword upon yours and when you are both in measure; circle your Sword with the turn of the wrist. If he does not ward, strike him in the face, and you will not need to do anything else. But, if he wards, you find the Swords in contact. You then affront strongly upon his Sword, so that he should affront. If and when he comes to affront; you circle coming with the circle below his hilt, and do the effect of the picture turning the body, as above, to wound him in the body, where he is not aware. Having done the effect of the present picture, then return outside of measure safely, as in the other lessons.

Once again, this lesson adds an additional dimension to the previous inquartatas. *As the other two, it involves the fencer holding the outside guard over-extended, permitting the opponent to circle the sword and make their attack with the inside counterguard. The fencer responds with the circle and extends the arm holding their guard firmly. If the opponent's defense or warding is insufficient, the under hand thrust is driven home. But if the opponent wards with the strength against the fencer's affront, the fencer lets go of the opponent's bind and circles under the opponent's sword. The opponent's will fall to the fencer's inside. The* inquartata *is then delivered in either of the previous ways described above.*

Lesson 22: The Artificial Way of Striking in the Body Affronting the Swords

In the past lessons I have shown the way of the *Inquartata*, that is to say affronting the Swords on the outside to go wounding on the enemy's inside. Now, it is to carry the Swords on the inside and wound on the outside, to this I shall speak briefly. As you are butting with the enemy; affronting strongly with the blade of your Sword, holding the point to the face, and with your forte upon the enemy's Sword. You shall judge when you affront his Sword. Take note, if you are stronger than him give an under hand thrust, either to the face, or to the body, which he will not be able to ward. But, if he is stronger than you, you must circle your Sword under his hilt. When his sword falls to the ground, you will likewise hold a point from which he shall not able to defend. In that time passage somewhat without peril, and set your left hand on his hilt, you then wound him with three or four points, which he will not be able to avoid. Then return outside of measure safely, as above.

The affront is the act of pushing the opponent's blade farther to the inside or outside, and is key to Giganti's feint. In all of Giganti's feinting techniques, if the opponent fails to use strength against the affront the under hand thrust is forcefully pushed through. If the opponent meets the affront with strength, the fencer releases the opponent's sword and circles to make a different attack. The strength applied by the opponent to their sword is used to defend the fencer, as when the fencer releases their guard, the opponent's weapon will quickly move out of a useful line of attack. Lesson 22 illustrates the effect of this play. This play begins with the fencer in an inside counterguard strongly binding against the opponent's outside guard. If the opponent does not sufficiently resist, the under hand thrust is driven home. If the opponent resists, the fencer releases the bind, causing the opponent's sword to move to the fencer's outside. In this time, the fencer circles into an outside counterguard, passages, and siezes the opponent's hilt. During this action, the fencer delivers the under hand thrust, and potentially several more afterward, as Giganti suggests.

Lesson 23: The Way of Playing with the Single Sword Against the Single Sword with the Resolute Point

In the Schools, there are many, who, when they intend to assault the enemy they throw the Point, Over hand thrust, or Cut with lusty resolution. All given without regard for time with fury & the greatest violence; thus soiling and setting common disorder upon all players and fencers. Thus, it is necessary for you to know in such occasions the way to defend yourself. When you set to guard the enemy's Sword with yours extended in action and outside the measure, it behoves you to have a narrow quick step. Beat the enemy's Sword with your forte in the time when he throws: a point, either Over hand or Under hand thrust, or other high cut. Quickly lengthening your step throw your point at him, wounding him either to the body or face. Quickly return backwards with the foot in front, from where you first sprang, leaning your Sword on his to secure it. In such a way, that it is impossible for him to wound you, without circling. If he circles, you turn your wrist to the outside, turning to beat the enemy's Sword with your forte. Lengthening your step, you throw a point at him, and then wound him. Quickly returning backwards with the feet, as above, securing yourself with your Sword in contact with the enemy's. If he turns re-circle anew, then you always turn to do the same.

This lesson is more useful, beautiful & you have it in two times, in which you are able to do first, before the enemy to has the time to do even one. The first which is the warding the other is the wounding. The which, as I observe, should be agreeable to you.

In this lesson Giganti gives a warning about the poor techniques that can develop in a practice setting where there is often little fear of mortality and fencers can be unduly reckless. Giganti warns that this manner of practice is 'soiling and setting common disorder upon all players and fencers.' *Modern practitioners of fencing can easily forget that swordplay was in fact a mortal art, and reckless practice in schools often led to reckless practice when applying the art of defence in real combat. Giganti's advice is to enforce a proper sense of time on this type of opponent by using the basic techniques covered in lesson 1. The fencer is to defend strongly and then attack strongly, thereby forcing the opponent to defend and acknowledge the time enforced by the fencer.*

Lesson 24: Parrying the Under Hand Thrust when it Comes for the Chest with the Single Sword

Plate 16

From this Picture is seen the way of safely parrying the point when it comes for the chest & to wound in the chest. This is done in many ways: some step in distance, others stand in measure, others outside of measure: But, those who have recognition of the time and know how to parry well as my picture shows you, they will be able to parry in all of these ways. Take note, when you are in contact with your enemy's Sword and he steps to wound to the chest. You do this technique. In the same time follow the enemy's Sword with yours, lowering your point by raising the wrist, and parry with the same; step with your left foot against his right side and push his Sword out of the way. Wounding him in the chest holding your left hand upon the furnishing enemy's Sword. Then, having struck the under hand thrust by circling the Sword neatly as described above, return backwards outside of measure.

This play begins with the opponent in an inside counterguard covering the fencer in an outside guard. As the opponent binds and comes into measure, the fencer raises the hand and drops the tip. This catches the opponent in the middle of circling and pushes his sword to the fencer's outside. In essence, this creates a hanging outside counterguard, with the tip below the hilt. This guard is given more strength as the fencer passages the inside foot forward and throws the point at the opponent's torso. Giganti's text also notes that in the same time as the passages and throws the inside hand to grasp the opponent's hilt; or the opponent's forte as is seen in the picture.

Lesson 25: The Point to the Face Turning the Wrist

Plate 17

You learn from this picture a most beautiful way of wounding your enemy's face. It all consists in pressing the occasion. Standing with the Swords in contact, having permitted your enemy to parry your motion, you make him wary that you intend to circle his Sword. In the same time: turn your wrist, place your left hand to his hilt, increase your left foot. In that time, you give it in the face; as is seen. This is impossible, for him to ward when you have done this properly. When you have given that, you must increase with your left hand upon the end enemy's Sword. Re-circling the Sword, you will then be able to throw at him two or three under hand thrusts where you wish. Then, return backwards outside of measure, always holding your Sword against his, as above.

This play begins with the fencer in the outside guard, which the opponent having just covered an attack with an inside counterguard. Instead of circling, the fencer performs four actions in the same time. The fencer following the motion of the opponent's ward to the inside passages the inside foot forward, places their inside hand to the opponent's hilt, inclines the body further to the outside, and inclines the head to the inside. In doing this, the fencer throws an under hand thrust at the face. It is important that the fencer pushes their sword well to the outside to make space for the opponent's sword to pass over fencer's shoulder between his head and sword .

Lesson 26: The Counter Circle in Distance

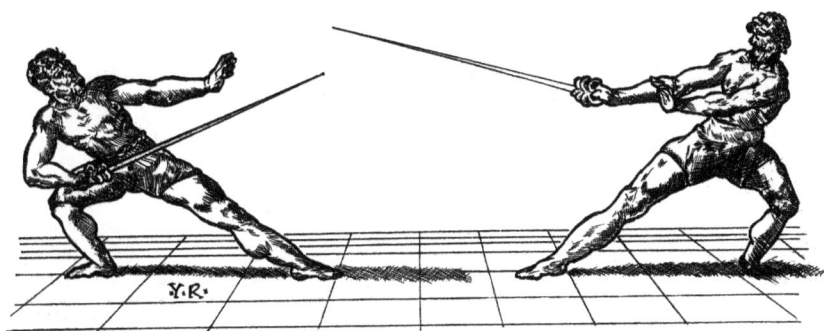

Plate 18

Plate 19

This is a similar counter circle, in distance with one whom happens to be forward with the left foot & who wants to step with *Inquartata*. I have shown with these pictures the posture & wounding. In order that it would be possible for you to understand clearly the doing of this technique (in which he comes to bind you with the left foot), so that you will be able to stand in guard as you see in this picture, giving the opportunity to your enemy of throwing at your body. If he should be a valiant man, he will step with the feet nimbly & turn his wrist strongly, in the way of *Inquartata*, for warding himself from your Sword. You in the same time that he steps, re-circle your Sword under his endings, lowering your torso, as you see in the present Picture. In this way, you will be able to wound him in the face before he can wound you. Instead, while he carries his foot forward wanting to step, he will not able to ward. But, if you want to achieve the effect of this picture you must first of all exercise the techniques in these two posts well.

Like the cuts, Giganti only briefly touches on how to defend against an attack starting from an inverted stance (i.e. inside foot forward) – as Giganti states in the last lesson of this book, he has saved detailed examination of fighting with the left foot forward for his Libro Secondo*.... As a result, some explanation of the opponent's actions and intentions is required, and as Giganti mentions in the text, both* "posts" *need to be practiced. The opponent, beginning in an inverted stance in an outside guard, extends his arm; in the same time, the opponent twists the wrist into the inside guard while passages the outside foot forward and to the inside. The intention is to use the momentum of the long movement of the sword and passaging of the body to beat the fencer's sword to his inside and throw the under hand thrust.*

The fencer's response relies on the fact that, while the opponent's attack carries a great deal of force, it is slow and difficult to alter. The fencer circles the opponent's sword, ideally, just before the swords make contact. At the same time, the fencer bends his back leg and moves the inside foot further to the rear, to drop his torso further back and gain more distance and time. Once this is done, the force of the opponent's forward movement should cause him to run on the end of the fencer's sword. Nonetheless, an outside long under hand thrust is easily thrown by the fencer if this does not occur.

Lesson 27: The Way of Playing with Single Sword when the Enemy has Sword and Dagger

Plate 20

I will show to you with this picture the parrying and wounding with the single sword against an enemy who has Sword and dagger. Standing with the right foot in front, a proper step, the torso held back, and the Sword forward nimble to parry & wound when it should be time. It does not help to be the first to throw, for you do so in peril, as, when you have thrown at your enemy he may be able to parry your under hand thrust with the dagger, and you would not be able to parry his. But, if he should be valiant man, you are to stand in guard as I said above in the action of parrying, showing hesitance to him, so that he will throw freely. While he throws, you will parry lustily with the forte of your Sword. You will throw the under hand thrust at the face. Because he throws at you strong and long and while he is throwing, he sends his dagger far off. Thus you will give it to him with a sure hand, and, quickly having given it, you will return back outside of measure, holding your Sword to his, in the way described above. Every time, when he throws, you will do the same. Take care not to throw at his body, which shall not be safe. After which he, who has the Sword and dagger, shall be much more ardent against the one, whom is retiring with single Sword. Thus, he is thinking to strike with as many under hand thrusts as he wants to. But, he shall come to disorder throwing at you with no other thought but that. But, you standing in your proper guard, are able to parry securely and strongly; always wounding your enemy in the face. Returning safely outside the measure, with your Sword upon his.

But, if your enemy circles his Sword to the inside; you turning your wrist will parry, and you will throw strongly, as I have said. If you happen to see that he is attempting to fall upon you as you throw yourself backwards, you will throw at him in the time in which he will move to come forward. If he happens to find himself in guard with your Sword on his, he will greedily parry first with the Dagger and then go to wound. In that time which you see he is lowering his dagger to parry, you quickly circle your Sword over the dagger to the way described in Lesson 28. Quickly, you return outside of measure with your Sword on his. Though take care, that if he should happen to stand in the same guard [as you,] you must not throw. If he is strong, you will not see any other time in which to throw than the time in which he will not be able to wound you, as it was described above when I dealt with the time and measure. If he is standing in guard waiting for fear or by applying the art of deception, you must keep yourself outside of measure, with your Sword upon his. Circling to parry and wounding securely following the opportunity.

Giganti introduces the sword and dagger, however, the fencer is using a single sword against the opponent armed with sword and dagger. Giganti's advice focuses on the defence with the forte against the opponent's sword followed consistently by throwing an under hand thrust at the face and then retiring in order to prevent the opponent from using the advantage of the dagger. Giganti also uses this technique to frustrate the opponent, who will be forced to attack more ardently against the fencer, thereby forcing the opponent to disorder himself by attacking more forcefully. The fencer then, in the opportune moment, strikes the opponent. The manner in which the fencer will successfully attack the opponent is not laid out mechanically – it is conceptual. When the opponent has thrown the under hand thrust (to which the fencer wards, parries with the forte, and throws an under hand thrust in response), the fencer will hold the counterguard and the opponent will be forced to use the dagger in order to bind the fencer. At the same time, the fencer has the opportunity to circle the dagger and continue to bind the opponent's sword. If this is not possible or fails, the fencer retires and continues the pattern of defence until another opportunity presents itself.

Lesson 28: The Parry of the Long Under Hand Thrust which Comes for the Face with Sword and Dagger[*]

Plate 21

To achieve the effect of the present picture, it behooves you to hold the guard in the manner that you know.[†] It behooves you to hold it a just & firm pace, with the arms nimble to ward and wound when the opportunity appears & the dagger to the guard of the enemy's sword. If you see that your enemy wants to throw a long under hand thrust against your face, you parry with the edge dagger & wound in the same time under the right arm. Which, if done in the same time he will only be able to parry with difficulty. But, to achieve the said effect, that he cannot parry, it is not enough of

---

[*] If the tone of this lesson seems unusual, it is because it was translated from the French 1619 edition of Giganti's *Scola over Teatro...* by Kim Reynolds.
[†] The posture described in lesson one.

know only these skills: it also behooves you need nimbleness in its use. Knowing you must take a firm guard, with the right foot in front, the left foot well firm supporting all the body, & Nevertheless, at the same time in such a manner with the opportunity offered to advance or retreat hastily, holding always the point of your sword against the face or the chest of the enemy, & the dagger raised, according to the placement of the enemy's sword. The body, rather than forward, is held back, with the eye lively & sure, and ardently without any fear of the enemy. If you maintain such a guard, when the enemy throws at you a sudden thrust, or a cut to the face, you parry with the edge of the dagger, throwing in the same time a thrust, as you see the effect in the picture. But, be aware to parry securely, keeping back the head and the torso. And, in parrying eagerly throw your long under hand thrust in the same time. Because, by parrying first and wanting to give the blow after, you gain nothing because the enemy can remove his arm & body, also he has time to parry & you will remain in danger. But, if you parry & throw in the same time, you will deliver the long under hand thrust underneath the cover of his sword while he comes forward. If this is done with dexterity & in time, he cannot defend well. Having thrown the long under hand thrust, you hold the left foot firm to retire backward out of measure.

For you to retire securely, it behooves you, after having given the blow, to retire first the head & the body, then the leg. Because, if you retire the leg first, the head & all the body remain forward in peril, without power to return out of measure. Throwing the long under hand thrust long & firm, in such a way that one cannot withdraw is of no value.

Thus to parry with the effect of the said picture, it behooves to learn the practice, so that seeing the enemy wants to throw, you throw as well in the same time, ensuring that you reach him first, even if he makes the first throw.

Giganti's manner of instruction changes considerably in his discussion of Sword and Dagger. Rather than discussing the precise mechanics of specific plays, he focuses more on tactics. As observed in lesson 4, Giganti relies on the techniques of single sword to instruct the mechanics of sword and dagger. As a result, Giganti is able to engage in a more abstract discussion. For example, the targeting of sword work becomes much more freeform. Rather than advocating precise targets on the opponent's body, Giganti frequently refers to targeting the "uncovered" parts of the opponent's body, whatever they may be. In the coming sections on the artificial guards it becomes clear that another reason for the vague language of Giganti's sword and dagger lessons is that there are more guards than the two in the single sword section of the book. Certainly, these two basic guards are still significant, but, in the coming pages Giganti adds three additional artificial guards, which vary the starting place of the plays significantly. The vague language of Giganti's sword and dagger lessons are an attempt to encompass the growing number of possible guards. In so doing, Giganti implies that when practicing, the fencer should endeavour to try all the various guards with all the various plays in order to gain 'knowledge of the guards.'

It is important to refer back to lesson one, where Giganti discussed the proper stance and guard with the sword and dagger. The difference between the guards of the single sword and the sword and dagger relate to the left hand. The dagger is held with the hand fastening the grip of the dagger and the thumb running along the upward facing flat of the blade. If there is a ring or guard (as opposed to a dagger with only quillions) these are meant to protect the fingers and are held on the opposite side from the thumb.**

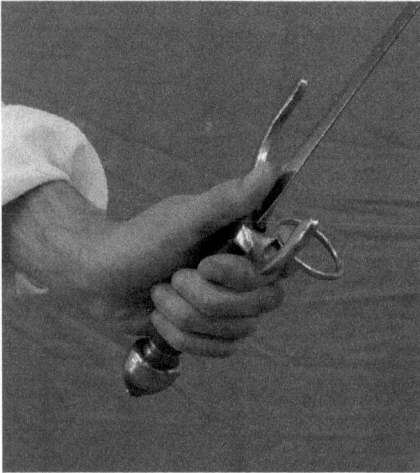

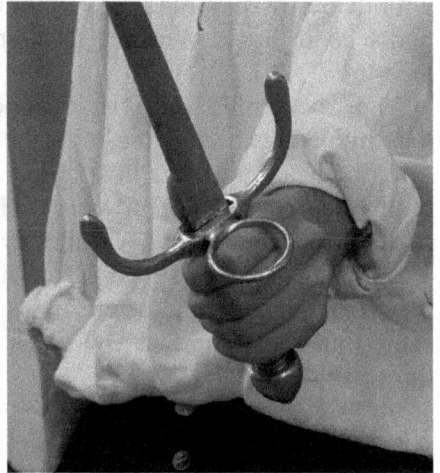

The inside arm and dagger is extended (but never locked) directly towards the opponent's sword. When this is done the proper use of the dagger is quickly developed from instinctual body movements. In addition, if the dagger is not held at full extension the dagger will not have time to respond to incoming attacks.

---

* Aligned with the blade of the dagger as evident in plates 29, 34, 36, 41, and 42.

All parries with the dagger conform to a rule of thumb: the dagger will always have the thumb facing towards the fencer's body, regardless of whether it is pointed upward or downward. This lesson introduces the first parry with the dagger. The first parry (high inside line) is performed by moving the still extended arm up and to the inside of the fencer's body. To ensure safety, the fencer's head is also leaned to the inside. The instinct to use the dagger in a side-to-side motion should generally be avoided, primarily because such motion transmits momentum onto the opponent's blade that can be used in a quick circling by the opponent's sword. Instead, the forward motion of the dagger toward the opponent's hilt is sufficient for a proper defense. For those new to fencing with the dagger, this movement may seem counter-intuitive. For the techniques of Giganti's system of sword and dagger to be properly understood fencers will need to take a leap of faith. In spite of the short movements of the dagger, these motions are sufficient to defend the fencer against an incoming under hand thrust.

The play begins with both the fencer and opponent begin by holding an outside guard. The opponent then uses their dagger to attempt to bind the fencer's sword to the fencer's outside. The fencer's sword is bound to the opponent's inside, and the opponent then throws the under hand thrust at the fencer's head. The fencer parries the opponent's sword with the dagger and throws the long underhand thrust to the opponent's right armpit.

The use of time in this, and subsequent, lessons also demonstrates a departure from the manner in which time is used in the single sword techniques. Here Giganti suggests that this technique is best delivered before the opponent's attack – mechanically this makes sense as it gives more distance, and thus time, for the fencer to make their attack. What Giganti fails to put into words (but includes in the illustrations) is that the fencer also has to avoid the opponent's dagger with the sword and throw an under hand thrust in the same time. It seems likely that Giganti's advice of pre-empting the opponent in throwing the thrust is the manner in which the opponent's dagger is avoided; however, a circling of the dagger can also work.

The first dagger parry

   This lesson relies on a simple attack using the dagger to clear the opponent's sword and then delivering a simple attack with the sword, which Giganti does not articulate in a separate lesson. This is unfortunate, as it seems to be a staple of fighting with sword and dagger and the foundations of Giganti's teachings; however, this attack can be extrapolated by understanding the opponent's intention in this play. This simple attack uses the dagger to make an opening and the attack is delivered to the uncovered part of the opponent. One of the reasons that Giganti makes no specific reference to it is that the simple attack must be able to be adapted to any possible guards of the sword, which Giganti himself has said are infinite. In learning Giganti's sword and dagger technique it is useful for fencers to practice this simple attack before practicing the techniques described in this lesson. To do this, the opponent is to stand in guard as the target, varying the location of the sword; the fencer then practices binding with the dagger (in all of the four basic dagger positions contained in this and the next two lessons) and throwing the under hand thrust at the opponent's uncovered areas – for this particular lesson, the exposed left flank.

   Once the simple attack is understood and practiced the action of this and subsequent lessons will become clearer. This attack will be an important concept as the discussion moves to the use of "artifice" in sword and dagger work, which emphasizes uncovering parts of the body to invite the enemy to make a predictable and simple attack to the uncovered areas. The fact that Giganti takes the readers knowledge of the simple attack for granted suggests an inherent amount of fencing knowledge possessed by the audience of Giganti's work.

Lesson 29: The True Way of Parrying the Under Hand Thrust if it Comes for the Left Flank

Plate 22

In the present picture, it behoves you to set as in that of above.* If your enemy designs to throw at your left flank, you must stand with your dagger toward the Guard of his Sword. In the same time that he throws, you must parry with the edge of the dagger. You must wound the enemy in his Sword shoulder at the same time. Actually, you would be better to more nimbly throw first, before he will throw his under hand thrust, being vigilant with your eye and mind, gathering in your torso. In that time when you see, that he wants to throw his, you must throw yours at his shoulder. Having parried his in that time, thus he is not able to parry yours; for which you will wound in that time when he is coming forward, as it is seen in the

---

* Giganti is referring to his description of the Guards of Sword and Dagger in Lesson 1.

picture. Having thrown the under hand thrust, return backward outside of measure, in the same way as the first picture of Sword and Dagger.*

This play is similar to the one described in lesson 28; however, in this play the opponent binds with the dagger in order to throw the point at the fencer's left flank. This gives Giganti the opportunity to illustrate the second dagger parry. The second parry (low inside line) is performed by turning the arm over so that the thumb turns towards the fencer's outside and finally comes to rest below the hand.

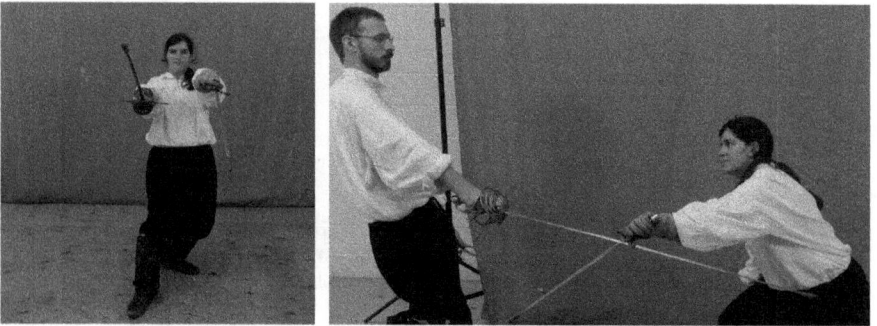

The second dagger parry

Both fencer and opponent begin in an outside guard. The opponent then uses their dagger to attempt to bind the fencer's sword to the high outside (using something resembling the first dagger parry). The fencer's sword is bound to the opponent's inside -- the opponent then throws the under hand thrust at the fencer's left flank. The fencer parries this with the second dagger parry and throws the under hand thrust. As with the previous play, the fencer ideally will understand his opponent's intentions and throw first.

* Lesson 28.

Lesson 30: The Way of Parrying a Point if it Comes for the Right Flank with Sword and Dagger

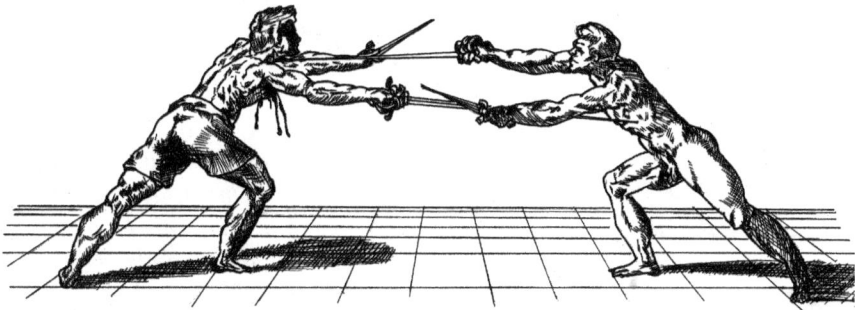

Plate 23

As you see in this picture, if you were to appear in the same guard as described above and in this case your enemy could come to bind you with his Sword low intending to wound you in the right flank. It behoves you to lurk with your sword arm and stand in the third guard* – in order to do an over hand thrust with the point of your Sword against his face or body – with the Dagger somewhat low and the arm toward the guard enemy's Sword. As the enemy throws the point to your flank, you throw the over hand thrust for the enemy's Sword shoulder in the same time that you parry.

---

* This inspired the use of numbered dagger parries in the interpretation of the text, as this lesson does introduce the third of the dagger parries or guards. However, Giganti's meaning is unclear.

You see the effect from the picture. Actually, it would be best done, to throw yours first, as soon as you see your enemy attempting to throw his point, because in this way you will more easily wound him. Quickly, having given the under hand or over hand thrust, return backward outside of measure.

These are the four sorts of ways of woundings, and parries of under hand & over hand thrust. All go in a similar way, that is to say to parry and wound in one same time. Always heeding in the carrying of the feet as you throw the under hand thrust, to increase somewhat with the right foot, holding the left foot firmly to the ground. Take care, keeping the left foot firmly to the ground appears a difficult task at first, but, with exercise you shall come to it easily.

In this lesson, the opponent makes a simple attack with the sword and dagger to the outside flank of the fencer underneath the sword. Both the fencer and the opponent begin in the outside guard described in lesson 1. The opponent binds by using the first parry with the dagger, which lifts the fencer's sword and moves it to the fencer's outside. The fencer responds with the third parry of the dagger (described below) and circling the sword and throwing an outside under hand or over hand thrust (depending on where the enemy is uncovered) all in the same time. This attack both binds and delivers the under hand thrust to the fencers outside. This lesson gives the opportunity to introduce the third parry with the dagger. The third dagger parry (low outside) is typically used with the over hand thrust; otherwise the fencer's sword and dagger may interfere with each other. Conforming to the rule of thumb (i.e. with the thumb towards the fencer's body) the inside hand is pushed downward and to the outside. According to the illustration this parry is conducted with the tip of the dagger pointed upward and to the outside. However, this parry relies heavily upon the fencer throwing the under hand thrust to their outside in order to permit the dagger to fully cover the fencer's outside. This particular parry is also problematic for taller fencers facing shorter opponents, as the taller fencer will find it difficult to lower the dagger far enough to catch their opponent's sword. In order to overcome these issues of height an alternative of the third parry is to conduct the parry with the dagger point downward in a fashion similar to the second dagger parry, merely held to the outside of the body rather than to the inside.

Giganti concludes this lesson with advice to incline towards the opponent's inside when throwing the point, in order to support the action of binding with the dagger and to slip away from the enemy's sword, similar to the movement introduced in lesson 7.

The third dagger parry

Alternative third dagger parry position

Lesson 31: The Way of Parrying the Point of the Sword and Dagger to the Face

Plate 24

For to want to do the technique and put in effect all which this picture shows you, it is necessary that you stand in this same guard. In order to accomplish this effect, Seeing the enemy coming to throw an under hand thrust at your face, you must parry with the edge of your dagger and thrust the under hand forward to his flank in one time. Therefore, take care when you see the enemy's Sword point to your face, hold your dagger somewhat wide of that in order to give him time to throw at you. When he throws, you must parry with the Dagger and turn the head somewhat, throwing it from the path of his Sword. In that time when you parry, you wound him with the point to the flank, which shall be uncovered, and the nearer to be wounded. Having wounded him, you must quickly return backwards in the way described.

Once again both fencer and opponent begin in an outside guard described in lesson 1. The opponent this time attempts a simple attack by binding inward with dagger parry three and throwing a high under hand thrust to the face. This is met with the dagger parrying in fourth and the head leaned to the inside. At the same time, the fencer circles the sword and delivers an inside under hand thrust to the opponent's outside flank.

This play gives Giganti the opportunity to introduce the fourth and last dagger parry. The fourth dagger parry is performed by the fencer moving their left arm upward and to the outside of the body. As with the first parry the fencer moves the head away (in this case to the inside) from the enemy's sword.

The fourth dagger parry

The actual mechanics of the play are simple. However, Giganti introduces the concept of artifice to his sword and dagger techniques. Giganti's admonishment that: 'when you see the enemy's point Sword to your face, to hold your dagger somewhat wide of that in order to give him time to throw at you.' This the basis of Giganti's artifice. By uncovering a part of the body, the fencer encourages the opponent to throw their point with full commitment.

Lesson 32: The Way of Parrying the Cut to Your Head with Sword and Dagger

Plate 25

As you see, you learn from this picture how to parry the cut with the Dagger, when it is directed to the side of your head. It behoves you to stand in the guard of the first lesson. If your enemy comes to throw a cut at you to your head, you must go to encounter him with the edge of your Dagger. In that same time, you must throw your point at the enemy's face, and increase somewhat forward with the right foot. You must do these three things together, which you can observe the effect in the picture. It is best used for large Cuts, which go to kill and do not have half-force. While the enemy raises the sword to throw the Cut, throw at him your under hand thrust at his face. This is best so that his head will retire somewhat backwards, he is wounded in the eye, and it will turn the power of his Cut. To want to do this effect you must do the technique with ardour, not fear his

Sword, nor the enemy. You must know how to parry well with the Dagger. You must know how to throw a good true and long under hand thrust. Guard against parrying the Cut with the flat of the Dagger, which should the Cut be strong, it may hurl your Dagger from your hand, and you will be wounded in the head. But, if you parry it with the edge, holding the arm extended, you will not be in peril. Having thrown the point, you must return backwards outside of measure, as above.

This play is similar to lesson 16, except here the dagger is being relied upon completely for the defence. The timing of this lesson is similar to the single sword lesson 16. Here, the fencer launches the under hand thrust when the opponent moves their sword out of line in order to build up the momentum for the swing. As Giganti says this works best for large slow cuts. The under hand thrust typically stops the opponent's attack, but if delivered late or facing a tighter and faster cut the dagger will be required to defend. Parrying a cut with a dagger is a difficult task. As Giganti notes, the fencer should pay special care to parry with the edge of the dagger as opposed to the flat. This is because of the way the hand works – to use the flat of the blade would mean that only the tension of the fingers would absorb the force of the blow. Use of the edge permits the structure of the hand itself to help absorb the blow. Although not mentioned by Giganti, using the blade of the dagger to channel the force of the blow in to the quillions is another precaution that helps in parrying cuts with the dagger.

Lesson 33: Of the Way of Parrying a Back Hand Blow with the Dagger

Plate 26

As you can see from this picture, it is learned how to parry a back hand blow, which comes against the face. It behoves you to set in the guard of the first lesson with the Dagger high and strong. As you see the back hand blow coming; go encounter it with the edge of the Dagger. In one time increase somewhat your right foot, throw the under hand thrust at his flank, which shall be uncovered, which you can see the effect of the picture. Heed that all six these pictures are of one manner.* But, it behoves you to parry, and to wound in one time. If you delay from the parry to the wound, you will not do the effect. To do this effectively, you must exercise and practice. Having given the under hand thrust quickly return backwards outside of

---

* This refers to lessons 28 through 33.

measure.

This is to be heeded, which in these six lessons is most important and best, which in the Fence can be found. But, it is best done by holding the Dagger strongly. As you see the Sword coming against you either with the point or edge, go to encounter it with the Dagger. In that same time to throw the under hand thrust where the enemy shall be uncovered.

This play simply shows a fourth dagger parry to catch a back hand blow to the head. This lesson is a good example of Giganti's more abstract approach to sword and dagger. His advice on parrying a back hand blow does not add significantly to the previous lesson on parrying a cut to the head. Instead, Giganti uses this lesson to re-emphasize a point about timing. Giganti's point has been made earlier in the previous six pictures – the fencer must endeavour to parry with the dagger and throw the under hand thrust in the same time.

The opponent's raised dagger is curious, and no indication is given in the lesson as to why the dagger is raised.Presumably, the opponent began the attack by binding the fencer's sword high to the opponent's inside to clear a path for the back hand blow.This would mean that the fencer has circled their sword in the time preceding the parry with the dagger and throwing of the under hand thrust.This is not of critical importance to the lesson contained in this declaration, but some may want to practice this precisely for the sake of completeness.

Lesson 34: Point Thrown at the Body with Sword and Dagger

Plate 27

One whom delights in the profession of arms must first know how to bind the enemy, give the under hand thrust, and return in guard outside of measure. To desire to do this technique you must have knowledge of countering the guards and throwing the under hand thrust where you see your enemy uncovered. If he should be a little covered in the body, it behoves you to go to bind him smoothly with the Sword low holding your point against the enemy's body; with your Dagger to the guard of his Sword. As soon as you are in measure you must throw the Sword first, then the torso, and after the feet. You see the effect in this picture. This must be done, for if you throw the Sword arm and then the torso to give him the under hand thrust at his body, he will not be able to notice. The contrary is if you move the torso first and then to throw the under hand thrust, then he will be aware, able to parry, and respond in the same time. This way puts you in peril.

Then, having thrown the under hand thrust, you must quickly throw yourself backwards outside of measure, standing in guard with your weapons ready to parry and wound. Because, the enemy, finding himself wounded will become disconcerted when he will throw at you either the point or edge. You then must parry and wound in one time as is described to you in the first six pictures.* But, the importance of this picture consists (when having thrown) in knowing to return outside of the measure. In order to return safely, it is best (as I have said above) to carry first the head backwards, then shall come the torso, and the leg; because, if you throw the legs first, you would find yourself in peril either of falling or being wounded by your enemy. It follows then, for the head to go first; it must be kept in mind that this is one of the principle things, that you must learn.

Once again, Giganti uses his lessons to reiterate points made previously and to illustrate tactical concepts rather than illustrating mechanical plays. In this lesson Giganti emphasizes the issue of timing discussed in his previous lessons with the sword and dagger, as well as the importance of aiming for the uncovered parts of the opponent so critical to the simple attack. Giganti also begins to reintegrate his lessons on the under hand thrust from Lesson 3. Of the most significance is his elaboration on the order of the under hand thrust, which was omitted from lesson 3. It is important to note that within the time of the under hand thrust there are six separate phases. The first three deliver the attack by moving forward: arm, torso, and then leg. The last three withdraw back out of measure: torso, leg, and then arm. Additionally, he restates the importance of throwing the hand first before the torso so the weight of the body can be used in binding and attacking. In the lesson he demonstrates another problem of throwing the torso first – it fails to extend the fencer's forte *against the opponent's* debole; *this weakens the bind. He continues the discussion of the under hand thrust in more detail in the next lesson.*

---

* This refers to lessons 28 through 33.

Lesson 35: Throwing the Under Hand Thrust Whilst the Enemy is Moving

Plate 28

In the fence the principle things to be known are to discern the measure and time; those we will examine in this picture. As soon as you, with Sword in hand, go to counter your enemy, you must go bind him with the eye lively and weapons ready to parry and wound. In that time, observe whether he wants to wound you first or not. If you see he desires to be the first; give him the Time to throw. You meanwhile, go to parry and throw at him in the same time, as above. But, if you see he fears you & thus he is standing in guard waiting, go to bind him plain and smooth to that part where he is uncovered. As he shall be in measure, hold your Dagger towards the guard of his Sword. Throw first your point, then your torso, then your feet, holding the Dagger in front, so that if the enemy should throw in the same time, you will be able to parry, thus he should not be able to counter you or strike you neither. When you have thrown, you must return backwards out of measure in the way described. That is best for you, when you go to bind, to observe whether he will do one of these three things: whether he will throw, stand firm to parry, or move to one side or other in order to bring himself outside of measure. If he will throw or stand firm, when are in measure, it behoves you to do this in the way described in the present lesson. But, if he would move, retiring or moving in this, that, or whatever way; you throw a strong and nimble under hand thrust holding the feet while you bend. Because, while he is moving he cannot wound you in that time which you have thrown. Then return outside of measure as usual.

In this lesson, introduces a new tactical concept: the fencer is to note the opponent's objectives, such as whether they will attack, defend, or to move backward out of measure. Giganti also reiterates several of the tactical concepts already discussed, including being attentive and nimble with the weapons, ensuring that the dagger is pointed directly at the opponent's sword hilt, and the order of throwing the underhand thrust. He also reiterates his earlier advice on attacking the opponent any time in which the opponent is not throwing the point of their sword.

Lesson 36: Throwing the Point Above the Dagger

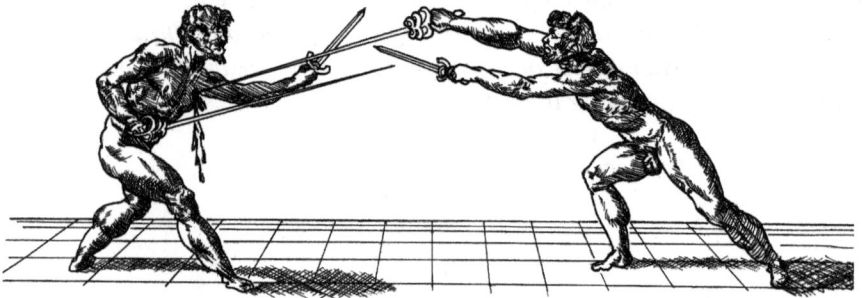

Plate 29

To wish to give an under hand thrust to one whom holds the Dagger low, it is best (as is seen in this picture) to go to bind him on the Dagger side. As you shall be in measure, you throw first the Sword and then the torso, with raising the wrist somewhat, in order to do the effect as is seen in the picture. Then, return backwards in the way described in the… [lesson 28]* picture. One, whom has already exercised throwing the sword first, then the

---

* This reference was left blank in the Italian 1606 edition. In the French-German 1619 edition it says "as in the present picture..." However, this makes little sense as this lesson contains no mention of how to withdraw other than this advice. I have instead referred back to lesson 28, which is referred to by other Rapier and Dagger lessons on how to retire out of measure.

torso, and then returning backwards nimbly, in the way described in the...[34] lesson . Whom, knows when to go to bind with the time. Who, if he is in measure, knows that he must throw where the enemy is uncovered. It is very difficult to parry it. Because, since that his Sword & Dagger cannot cover all, he is already uncovered in some part; it is best that you, when and where he is uncovered, wound in the aforesaid manner.

In spite of the somewhat long description for this play, the actual mechanics are simple. The fencer throws an under hand thrust to the opponent's inside shoulder using the dagger to bind the sword with a first dagger parry (high inside). The opponent (holding the dagger low) moves quickly to parry the attack with the dagger, in response the fencer turns the wrist into an over hand thrust and throws the forward leg farther to the outside, permitting the attack to bent around the dagger and wound the opponent's shoulder. The illustration seems to indicate that the opponent is struck while pulling his sword back to escape from the fencer's bind with the dagger. The remainder of the lesson reiterates the importance of time, measure, and retiring out of measure after throwing the point.

Lesson 37: Of the Guards in General

Many are the guards, that are able to be done, because each way of holding the Sword is a guard, as it has been said. All the guards are of value, when one has knowledge of the time and measure: And one whom is able to perform the artificial guards will always be able to deceive the enemy.

Giganti makes two important points here. The first, that these following plates describe additional guards other than the two simple guards described in lesson 1 and lesson 5. The second is that his system of fencing only describes only a small part of larger body of fencing knowledge.

Lesson 38: Artificial Guard with Uncovering the Left Part

Plate 30

The Artificial Guards are infinite, but, in my first book I shall set down only three. These guards show and offer a path to those who are knowledgeable of guards to put into practice as many of these as they may please.

The true and primary way of standing in an artificial guard is this: to uncover part of the body. All the other parts must be covered, so that it is impossible for the enemy to wound you except in that single part, as is seen in this picture. Here you uncover all of the left shoulder, so that the enemy should come to wound in the uncovered part. As he attempts to wound you, he shall be in peril; for as he will attempt to throw either the point or edge, you will be able to parry and wound him in one time. Increase with your foot, which accompanies the Sword, as you are parrying. Having thrown the under hand thrust quickly return outside of measure as above. These artificial guards are for studied men who have practiced well and have knowledge of time and measure; because when in these guards it is possible to do many things. First, above all, it is possible to go to bind the enemy. As you shall be in measure and he is caught in a moment as he was expecting something, it is possible for you to be able to wound him, where he is uncovered. Once he has thrown you are able to do many things: Such as to parry and to wound in one time, to parry and do a feint, a passage, or all that which you know to do in other guards that you have exercised. If your enemy standing in guard were to throw while he is distracted, you must parry and wound in one time; because, you will find him surprised. Quickly return backwards outside of measure. This guard deceives a great many: those whom are capable and those who are ignorant of weapons. For, when they see you uncovered, they throw at the part you have uncovered, as he has considered that there was no apparent danger, and, you easily parry & wound in the aforesaid manner.

Giganti begins this lesson by stating clearly that he is introducing three new guards, which he calls 'artificial.' The two basic guards rely on covering the body; these new guards rely on attempting to induce the opponent into attacking an area intentionally left uncovered by the fencer. However, this opening is only an illusion, and in spite of being uncovered the fencer is still well defended. This artificial guard has the fencer leaning their head to the inside while both sword and dagger are pointed wide to the outside, the sword hand being somewhat rotated upward toward neutral in spite of holding an outside line.

While not giving specific instructions of how it is to be done, Giganti claims that any of the techniques discussed in the sword and dagger section of his work are easily done from this guard. The practical exercise involves attempting each sword and dagger lesson from this guard and each of the other artificial guards.

Gary Chelak's interpretation provides an example of this guard combined with the techniques of Lesson 46; it also demonstrates one of the key techniques in the artificial guards. In this situation, the opponent seeking to bind the fencer's sword assumes an inside counterguard, binding with the sword and dagger in the first position in order to throw the under hand thrust at the fencer's left shoulder. In response the fencer draws the leading foot back to the rear foot and defend against the under hand thrust with the dagger to the low outside (i.e. the third dagger parry, see lesson 30). At the same time the fencer twists the wrist into an over hand thrust, turning the sword in the middle of the blade and making a wide circle with *the hand and the tip. The tip of the sword circles the dagger and then drops between the opponent's weapons, aimed downward at the opponent's chest. It is important when drilling and sparring with this play for the opponent to have the full intention of hitting with their attack.*[*]

---

[*] Gary Chelak, "Arteful Rapier & Dagger" (Class and Handout: WMAW 2004). Handout available at: http://tattershall.discoperta.com/pdf/WMAW04-handout-lowrez.pdf.

Lesson 39: Artificial Guard of Uncovering the Right Part

Plate 31

As you see, this is another artificial guard, which uncovers all your right side. The remainder of the torso is all covered so that the enemy cannot wound; but, one does not uncover the right shoulder. You are able to parry with the Sword or Dagger as desired and you are able to wound with the feet firm or else stepping with the feet as you retire commodiously. In this guard you are able to do many feints. These guards are good against those whom are willing to wound you & those who do not have the patience to wait to throw with the time and measure. When he sees you uncovered he will greedily set upon you without considering that there is much that you can do. Straight he finds his peril. It is good also against some, who after when they see better your business, they do a feint to you. You are able to parry better, than when you stand in a straight guard. You are more able to deal with the resolute point by carrying your torso backwards, parrying, and returning the torso, after which your points shall be nimble and long.

This guard is a variation on the basic inside guard with the sword hand palm upwards and to the inside. The primary difference lies in the tip of the sword being held to the outside to cover the outside shoulder and head – this posture exposes the fencer's right forearm and abdomen to the opponent; this is intended to induce the opponent to attack these uncovered areas. Giganti again claims that these guards can be used in several ways, largely leaving it up to the reader to figure out and practice the combinations of plates and guards.

Giganti specifically refers to the withdrawal of the leading foot in the same manner used by Gary Chelak in his demonstration and analysis of the artificial guards using Lesson 46. The opponent attacks in an outside guard with the dagger endeavouring to parry in the fourth position (described in lesson 31). The fencer conducts a wide circle with their sword underneath both the opponent's sword and dagger while at the same point drawing back the leading foot and the torso, and, parrying the opponent's sword with their dagger in position two (see lesson 29). The fencer's sword comes to rest in an over hand position between the opponent's weapons. If the opponent launched their attack with the proper force and intention they should run upon the fencer's tip; if not, the fencer can push forward and throw the over hand thrust.*

---

* Ibid.

Lesson 40: Artificial Guard of Uncovering the Body

Plate 32

In this other guard, you must uncover the body. Which your enemy will not be able to wound you, either from his Sword side, nor dagger side. When he goes to wound, you will throw forth in the waist so only that shall be uncovered. While he throws, you will parry and wound in one time, to either the right shoulder or face, as these are much closer. You are able in this guard to do some feints, stepping with the feet, and all things that have been learned in the other guards. This one is good against those throwing resolutely and without doing a feint. But, against those who have time and measure and who know how to throw a good resolute point and the feint, it is of no use; it is necessary for him to bind with your weapons. Seek to cover while the enemy's Sword is outside of measure, so as to be able to parry and wound without danger when the opportunity presents itself.

Giganti's third, and last, artificial guard is based loosely on the simple outside guard; however in this case the fencer holds their weapons high and with the sword tip inclined to the outside and the dagger point to the inside. This is meant to encourage the opponent to attack the fencer's hips or belly.

Gary Chelak's association of this guard with lesson 45 is clear as it forces the opponent into a low line attack. The additional distance the opponent's attack must travel in the low line also forces the opponent to attack with greater intention. This gives the fencer additional measure and time as they dominate the high line of the fight. It is the basic geometry of fencing found in lesson 18 of the single sword techniques, and indeed of almost every treatise on fencing. The use of the dagger permits a more secure defence against a low thrust. In response to the opponent's low under hand thrust, the fencer turns their sword into an over hand thrust, parrying with the dagger in the third position and drawing the leading foot and the torso backwards.*

The use of the artificial guards in modern sparring presents a problem in the practical application. Where this guard seems to be most effective in sparring is against fencers unfamiliar with Giganti's work. It is likely that this phenomenon would have been similar in the seventeenth-century. Giganti's system of fencing was to be used against a variety different of fencing systems and not merely against students of Giganti's system. This is confirmed in several places in the proceeding text when Giganti hints at the vast number of guards which he does not describe. While Giganti does not make specific reference to how to defeat the techniques of other masters (as Thibault does in his treatment of Fabris),† he does imply that alternative systems of fencing existed concurrently and came into conflict with each other. This implication, as well as the identification of the simple attack in lesson 21, suggests that there was a wider undocumented cultural body of knowledge regarding the martial arts in early modern Europe.

In modern practice, fencers who are familiar with Giganti's artificial guards are unlikely to be induced into attacking into them. The same is true for novice fencers, who will be hesitant to attack into any guard that seems unfamiliar. However, this is only the case if a fencer attempts to start a bout in one of these guards. The artificial guards can still succeed against both

---

* Ibid.
† Girard Thibault d'Anvers, *Academy of the Sword*, "Wherein is demonstrated by mathematical rules on the foundation of a mysterious circle, the theory and practice of the true and heretofore unknown secrets of handling arms on foot and horseback," Trans. John Michael Greer, (Chivalry Bookshelf, 2006). 240-5.

these types of opponents if the artificial guard is used in during the heat of the fight, when the opponent lacks the time to carefully consider the fencer's guard. In the seventeenth century, the adrenaline of an actual to-the-death fight with sword and dagger may have had a similar effect on the ability of the opponent to carefully consider the effect of a fencer's guard.

Lesson 41: The Feint with Sword and Dagger to Wound Above the Dagger

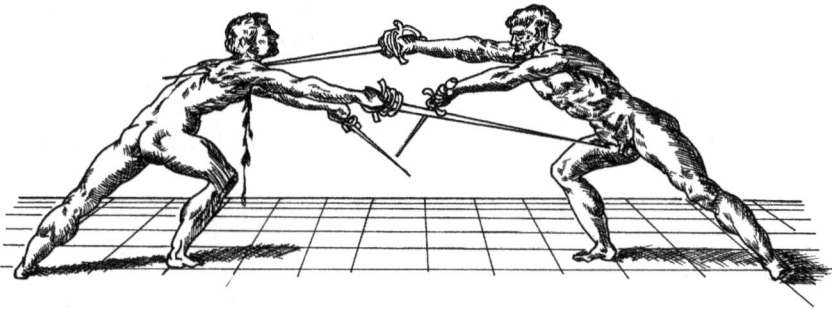

Plate 33

Thus, as the recognition of the time and measure are the principle foundations of the Fence; thus, the circle and feint are the ornaments of this same thing. The Circle constituted all in the wrist. The feint is the display of doing the same thing and not doing it. Nor can one do the Feint without circling; circling either above or below the guards of the Sword, above or below the point of the Dagger, or inside or outside. I cannot tell you how to throw the Feint, if I do not include the circle. The Feint is a mortal deception and cannot be recognized or withstood by persons of valour and professors of this science, without this above.

This is done in these ways. Giving the under hand thrust above the Dagger to the enemy's body or face, sometimes it behoves you to bind his Sword by lowering it below the Dagger, holding your Dagger to the guard of his Sword. As you find yourself in measure, you throw a resolute under hand thrust and then return backwards. If this comes to pass, you need do nothing else. But if he parries, you return to bind and as you should be in measure you throw the Point without lengthening the step, standing with the torso firm lowering the Dagger. While the enemy goes to parry that, in the lowering of his Dagger, you raise the point of your Sword with the circling of the wrist, then lengthening the step and torso. Since he will not be aware of this at all, you will wound him either in the body or face as you see in the Picture. So that it has this effect. It is best done with great nimbleness so that he shall not recognize between the resolute and the feint. Take care when going with the point of the Sword above the enemy's Dagger, to come with the Circle. When you have circled and wounded, which should be in one and the same time. Then return backward outside of the measure as previously stated, thus, you should be safe from the enemy's Sword.

Giganti reviews several concepts in the first part of this lesson, including the relationship between time and measure, circling, and feinting. While there is nothing new presented in this discussion, the reiteration acts as a reminder of the importance of these concepts to Giganti's system of fencing – just like the constant admonishments to 'return backwards outside of the measure.'

The technique described here is how to lead the opponent into a low line defence so that the sword can be circled over the dagger and an over hand thrust thrown. This is done by using a preceding attack to bring the opponent's sword into a low line. Through a bind with the dagger in the second position, Giganti lowers the opponent's sword and throws an under hand thrust for the face or body, forcing the opponent's dagger into the first position parry. Of course, as with all of Giganti's feints, this attack should be delivered with full intention, and, if this under hand thrust is successful, the rest of the play is not required and the fencer withdraws outside of the measure. If the opponent is successful in making a defence with the dagger, the opponent's dagger now rests in a high line and the fencer, maintaining the bind on the opponent's sword with the dagger, returns with the sword, throwing a low outside under hand thrust. This forces a radical movement of the opponent's dagger downward giving the fencer the opportunity to circle the sword above the opponent's dagger. The over hand thrust is then thrown at the opponent's chest.

Lesson 42: The Feint of Sword and Dagger Wounding in the Breast

Plate 34

This feint is done with the same rules of the previous one; it is not very different from the last, except, unlike the previous one, this one is low. In this, you shall have your Sword high and straight, which the enemy must in the throwing of your point raise his Dagger raising your arm somewhat more and the point of the Sword; this way of wounding is called Murdering the Dagger. If he does not parry, do not continue. But, if he parry's, standing with the step and feet firm, having more or less presented you the point. While he goes to parry you, come with the point of your Sword under the hilt of his dagger, circling the wrist & lengthening the step you wound him in the body where he is not nor aware. Then return in back outside of measure securing you as above.

In spite of Giganti's claims of this play being similar to the previous one, there are some significant differences. The intention of drawing the opponent's dagger out with an offensive action and then circling the sword around the dagger is similar. The movement is different – from a high feint to a line below the dagger parry. Another difference is that this is done all in a single attack, rather than a separate attack as a prelude. This feint is performed if the opponent successfully defends against a high line attack, likely to the face. The play contained in this lesson has the fencer launch an under hand thrust to the opponent's inside shoulder, binding the opponent's sword to their lower inside with the dagger in the second position. When the opponent parries the incoming under hand thrust with the dagger in the first position, the fencer circles underneath the dagger and throws an outside under hand thrust at their opponent's inside shoulder, holding the sword wide to bend around the dagger. If this attack lands, Giganti says 'do not continue.' However, if the opponent extends their dagger further to the high inside, the fencer circles below the dagger to deliver an inside under hand thrust at the opponent's outside shoulder between the sword and dagger.

The precise meaning of this term 'murder' – "scannatura" in Italian – is unclear. Tom Leoni has interpreted it to mean an attack against the opponent's neck, in accordance to one of the definitions found in Florio; however, the title of the lesson indicates it is an attack to the breast. This interpretation is contradicted by Ridolfo Capoferro's use of the word, which does not involve targeting the opponent's neck, rather Capoferro's scanntura is through the chest. Nor does Giganti make any reference to the neck in this lesson or lesson 41, and the blow pictured above, while near the neck, is in the torso. This suggests that the other definitions out of Florio of "murther" or "butcherie" are the ones intended by Giganti and Capoferro. This also suggests that Florio's use of throat cutting may have been to express the seeming negative connotation of the word.*

What is similar between the actions of the scannatura *depicted in Capoferro and Giganti is the movement of the fencer's body toward one side and the sword attacking to the other. In Capoferro's* scannatura *the motion has the fencer inclining their body to the inside with a passage and the sword delivered radically to the fencer's outside. Giganti's* scannatura *has the fencer moving their body to the outside while striking with the sword on the fencer's inside. This interpretation suits the action both of Capoferro's and Giganti's actions.*

---

* This can be an easy point to confuse in Capoferro, as the use of the word Scanatura comes after a plate in which there is obviously an attack to the throat, however, that picture is in fact for the previous lesson. Capoferro, 58-61.

Lesson 43: The Feint of Sword and Dagger to the Face Having circled the Sword above the point of the Dagger

Plate 35

To want to give an under hand thrust in your enemy's face in the first turn, it behoves you to do this Feint. It is at the same time most difficult, thus it is most beautiful. It behoves you then to bind the enemy from the contact of the Swords, holding the point of your Sword to the right side of his face. It behoves you to wait and see if he has the intention to wound you, otherwise he shall want to stand in guard to parry. If he remains in guard, you are to bind the point to his face. As he comes with the dagger obediently, you circle the point of your Sword above the enemy's dagger point. You will wound him, because he will not take care because his parry will have uncovered all. Having struck with the point, do as above.[*]

---

[*] i.e. to quickly return outside of the measure.

This is the most puzzling plays in Giganti's work. Part of the problem lies in Giganti's instruction: 'circle the point of your Sword with the wrist above the enemy's point dagger...' *and the opponent's final dagger position downward over the outside of the sword arm. Much of the problem lies in the Italian word* "sopra," *which has a number of potential translations into English, including:* "above," "over," "high," *or* "rising." *The play starts with the opponent in an outside guard and the fencer in the inside counterguard. The fencer then throws an under hand thrust at the opponent's face, to which the opponent parries with the dagger as their sword is bound to the fencer's outside. Logically, the opponent's should be using the fourth dagger parry, but, this is contradicted by the position of the dagger in the picture. Regardless, the fencer is to circle their sword over or to a place above the point of the opponent's dagger. The direct interpretation, as Leoni has done, suggests the fencer's sword is somehow lifted from the inside line over the dagger directly into the outside over hand thrust.* * *While this is possible, it still fails to explain the positioning of the opponent's weapons.*

The position of the fencer's sword in the picture is in an over hand thrust in the outside line, which could also be accomplished by circling the sword below the opponent's sword and dagger and having it come to rest above the opponent's dagger with the over hand thrust in the fencer's outside line. This action also potentially explains the opponent's final position in the plate. The downward circle forces the opponent's sword downward and to the fencer's outside; this is gathered and bound by the fencer's dagger in the third position. As the opponent relying on the dagger for the defense, they may instinctively follow the fencer's sword with the dagger bringing it to its position over the outside of the sword arm. As Giganti says this is a difficult play to execute – it is also a difficult play to interpret.

---

* Giganti, *The School or Theatre...* (2010) 47.

Lesson 44: The Parry of the Long Under Hand Thrust with the Sword by Carrying the Body Backwards

Plate 36

He whom can parry well is thus a master. I hold knowing how to parry well as the most important in the profession. Then, I want you to learn three ways of warding the long under hand thrust. Being in your guard, with the Sword in the high path, the torso forward, holding the body somewhat uncovered. Either standing in or out of measure, but never inside the measure. Being in measure, when you see him throw the under hand thrust, then carry your torso backwards parrying with the Sword, as you see in the Picture. When you throw yourself backwards, somewhat long to save yourself from the enemy's Sword point, keeping yourself thus far, he shall not be able to arrive at you. In the same time he is diminished with his torso bent, he is placed in disorder, and is only able to parry with difficulty. Then you will be able to wound him by lengthening the step and you are able to safeguard yourself, as above. Take care that while you are parrying you must return backwards standing strongly over your feet.

This play has already been discussed in the interpretation of lesson 11. A simple defence against a bind and under hand thrust by drawing the weight backward, bringing the torso backwards out of measure, and twisting the wrist into the opposite guard. This will effectively give the fencer the counterguard against the opponent. When the opponent's attack is spent the fencer then throws the under hand thrust at the opponent between the opponent's offensive and defensive times.

Lesson 45: The Parry with the Dagger Carrying the Torso Backwards

Plate 37

S tanding in the same guard as above, with the torso artificially forward, holding the Dagger toward your enemy's guard. As you shall be in measure and you see him throw his point at you; in the same time parry with the dagger and carry the torso backwards with retiring the forward leg. The Sword held nimbly to wound as you see in the Picture. You must stand with the feet strong and your Sword at liberty to be able to do many things before he returns to guard, because he, by throwing long and falling with the torso will give you the chance to strike where you will.

This technique is similar to that of the previous lesson by drawing the weight and the torso backward out of opponent's measure. The dagger is used instead of the sword to bind the opponent's weapon. From this position the fencer may throw the under hand thrust at where the opponent is uncovered.

Lesson 46: The Parry with the Dagger Carrying the Torso Backwards And wounding with the Sword in the same time

Plate 38

In the two previous pictures that parry with the [sword and] dagger, the torso is carried backwards and then wounding. They show that in two times, the one in the parry and the other in the wounding. Thus with this other Picture of mine, you see how to parry and wound in one time. The reason for this carrying of the torso backward is that you wish to be able to disconcert your enemy and to see better your business. Now then, setting yourself in the same guard as above with sword and dagger, with the torso forward bending the body. When you shall be in measure, let him throw at you. When he throws at you, you have to do three things in one time. That is to say: parry with the dagger, carry the torso backwards by plucking the forward foot back, and resting on the waist lengthen the arm and throw the point at his body: This way of parrying and wounding deceives the enemy, because it makes it impossible for him to defend himself. After you return outside of measure and you are safe, as it has been said.

As Giganti observes, this technique is similar to the previous plate, but it delivers the attack in the same time as the parry with the dagger. This technique is effective against an opponent who is throwing resolutely, as it relies on the opponent's forward momentum. Against an opponent's under hand thrust the fencer simultaneously parries the opponent's attack with the third dagger parry, draws the leading foot back to – or past – the rear foot, and extends and the sword in an over hand thrust. It is important that all three of these actions be done fluidly, as they all have an impact on each other. The sword must be raised in order to create room for the dagger to parry. The foot must be drawn back in order to shift the body backwards and to the inside in order to retire from measure and narrow the fencer's profile for the dagger parry to be successful.

Lesson 47: The Point to the Face Parrying with the Sword

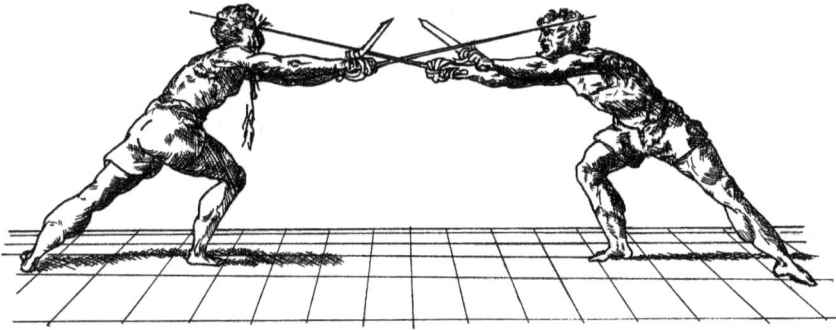

Plate 39

This picture shows a very useful point with the feet firm. It is good for those whom have excelled and have the knowledge to put it into practice, and it needs to be practiced. This is done in this way. It requires that your enemy throw an over hand thrust at your waist or else a point from his right. You parry with your Sword directing your point in the same time at the enemy's face, which he is not able to parry in the same time with his Dagger. Throwing at him in the time in which he throws. If he attempts to parry with the dagger, it shall beat his own Sword in* and the point to his face will remain. This lesson teaches nothing if not how wound in the face. If you throw at his body, he may be able to parry with his Dagger. This

---

* To the fencer's inside.

wants to be artificially done, so as to hide it from those who are knowledgeable. It is best to uncover your left side and to hold your Dagger low to give opportunity to the enemy, who will throw either to the face or above the Dagger, trusting that you will parry with your Dagger. While you, in the same time, ward with the forte of your Sword and increasing with your right foot, holding the point of your Sword against his face. If he wants to parry, he will tangle his Sword, so he will not be able to parry nor wound, as in the Picture. Having thrown the point, return backwards outside of measure, as above.

This technique is in response to any attack made by the opponent to the fencer's inside. Against such an attack, the fencer binds with the sword and throws an inside under hand thrust, supporting the attack with the dagger in position one against the opponent's under hand thrust or in position two against the opponent's over hand thrust. The high outside position of the opponent's sword hand prevents the opponent from using the dagger effectively in the defence, as it will only serve to trap the opponent's sword.

Lesson 48: The Passage of Sword and Dagger for Going to the Press and Wounding with the Dagger to the Face

Plate 40

Going to the press and wounding with the Dagger is done in many ways. It follows the opportunity in which others would retreat. Many go to the press because they miss, following the enemy they furiously step in. Others step from the choler, which have not the patience to play at the point of sword. Others step artificially to wound with the Dagger. In my first book, I write of only one artificial passage for wounding safely with the Dagger, which will be impossible for your enemy to offend you with neither sword nor dagger. This passage is done in this way. It behoves you to stand in a guard of this manner: resting with all the right side uncovered, to give opportunity to the enemy so that he throws resolutely, with either the point or edge. You will then parry with your Sword and step with the feet affronting him strongly with your Sword. Place your Sword to his Dagger arm, as you see in the Picture. Thus your enemy will not be able move either his Sword or Dagger. Then you make many eager stabs with the dagger. This lesson, when you have exercised it, is very safe.

Giganti, in general, warns against stepping inside of measure in order to go to the press. However, indicated by this lesson, Giganti does believe that advancing inside the measure can be successful. Giganti's second book covers the techniques of fighting from an inverted stance and going to the press. In theory, many of Giganti's techniques of the passage with the single sword could be classified as going to the press. But, Giganti chooses to avoid the detailed discussion of the press to simplify his first book, and, instead gives a handful of plates to promote the second book.

The fencer's starting position for this play is unclear. It could simply be an extended inside guard as seen in the feints. This play also could begin in the 'artificial guard of uncovering the right part' (described in lesson 39). For the purposes of this interpretation, an extended inside guard is assumed. The opponent throws an outside under hand thrust at the fencer's right side. The fencer wards with the outside counterguard and passages the inside foot forward with the dagger aimed at the opponent's face. This passage bolsters the strength of the bind as it inclines the fencer's body toward the inside. Additional security is gained by the fencer placing their sword along – or through – the opponent's inside arm, trapping both the opponent's weapons on the outside of the fencer's sword.

Lesson 49: The Point with Sword and Dagger Throwing from the side to the right Shoulder

Plate 41

One shall be a valiant man in this profession if he never sets in guard except when he is standing well outside of measure, so that he may consider the enemy's guard. He will go to bind him straight, smooth, and long to the uncovered part. When he shall be in measure you will throw at him in the way of the present picture, in which his right shoulder is uncovered. Take care to go to bind him to the side of your sword. If you shall see him standing in guard waiting; you will throw a strong under hand thrust in the way described by turning the wrist to side the enemy's sword, as is seen, Then having thrown the under hand thrust, you must return outside of measure as above.

This play begins with the fencer holding an outside guard covered by the opponent's inside counter guard. If the opponent does not throw the point, the fencer parries with the dagger in the fourth position at the same time the fencer raises their sword to shoulder level and pushes it far to their outside. The fencer's dagger pushes the opponent's sword into the fencer's bend. This permits the fencer to throw the point safely at the opponent's outside shoulder.

Lesson 50: The Passage with the Feet of Sword and Dagger

Plate 42

This Picture does not hold with the others, it is not a demonstration of what I have done in my first book. But, in the others, which I will set my hand to, if it is pleasing to God in heaven, I shall deal with the passage with Sword and Dagger, that is to say passage with the feet, since in this I do not treat of anything now except of the feet firm. Since, if one knows how to take the time it is possible to passage the feet. Then having done the passage to know the technique of circling the Sword and then safeguarding yourself, as you see in this Picture of the passage. Having circled your sword it is possible to give him many under hand thrusts and be safe by holding the Dagger toward the enemy's Sword. But, were the enemy to circle his Sword it would behove you to pursue it with your Dagger; in so doing, wound with the Sword. As you have given the under hand thrusts that you wish, you must return backwards outside of measure. For that one who knows to take the time properly and who steps with the feet, but, who does not know how to use the Sword, it would be as sad as to not know anything at all. Because by stepping, even in the instance to be able to wound, he will find himself in peril. Take note then, of when the enemy shall want to make his attack; because it is possible to find those who are courageous who, even if wounded, still want revenge and thus in their fury they will throw at their worst causing you to be in danger of being wounded or killed. Now, when your enemy steps forward you are able to parry his under hand thrust, as you see in the picture, you shall find yourself in great danger if you do not know how to circle the sword. Knowing the combat at the half Sword, to be able to return backwards, and place yourself in safely, shall be reasoned in my other books, if it pleases our lord God.

T H E   E N D

This last lesson of Giganti's book is another promotion for his subsequent works. The primary intention of this lesson seems to be a warning of the dangers of fighting at the half sword, thus giving Giganti's readers motivation to purchase his second book. Similar to lesson 48 Giganti avoids an elaborate discussion of close fighting and only gives the reader a few examples to avoid major lacunas in his readers skills.

A Modern Training Syllabus

METHOD

The master-student relationship is the most common image brought to mind when learning any martial art. There are some advantages to be gained from this system of training – primarily it is effective in the transfer of skills from the master to the student. This system of training also provides a formalized environment and codes of behaviour meant to control divergent or disruptive personality types. However, above all else, the master-student system of training is a well-proven business model, taken from the study of Eastern Martial Arts forms. But, the master-student system is not the only model with which to study the Western Martial Arts (WMA) or Historical European Martial Arts (HEMA).

I have been studying various forms of WMA for 15 years without having a formal instructor at my disposal. With the exception of the occasional weekend conference, I have been largely self-taught. The result is that I have developed a different training method than the master-student paradigm. My training system takes the format of a history seminar, with a specific master's manual playing the role of the literature being discussed. The training group as a whole is encouraged to propose and test interpretations of the text. The class approaches the text in a cautious trial and error fashion. While this approach is slower than the traditional paradigm, it does give the individual members of the study group a greater critical understanding of the subject, as they have seen why certain interpretations work and why other interpretation do not.

The nature of WMA and HEMA bring additional complexities to the master-student system, which can overshadow the advantages of this training arrangement. One of the most obvious is availability, within the current state of WMA there is often no instructor available. Another significant issue is that of inflexibility – because of the codification of interpretation, behaviour, and curriculum in the formalized master-student system, it is not easy for these systems to adapt to change. This is made more complex by the need of the master-student system to define orthodoxy. In short, the authority wielded in conventional training systems is not suited to the fact that Western Martial traditions have a broken lineage with the past, and, that all interpretations are just that – interpretations.

The problem is that the study of western martial traditions is one of the interpretation of historical documents. The codification of orthodoxy conflicts with the increasingly refined understanding of these complex systems. The master within the traditional paradigm has a difficult time changing their overall system when ongoing scholarship, training, and learning add more understanding to the documents being studied.

The seminar approach directly addresses these issues of on-going scholarship and re-interpretation. The author of a particular work becomes the master and their writings become the orthodoxy of the class. This acknowledges the break in the lineage of the art and permits multiple interpretations. This also permits interpretations to be reappraised and changed without having to battle personal egos, codified behaviours, formalized curriculums, and institutional hierarchies. With the identification of the author as the absent master, the group as a whole can examine the manual in question, each member bringing differing perspectives and skill sets to the problem of understanding the master's teachings.

This approach does have its drawbacks: it is much slower in developing skills and involves more work on the part of the students. It can also be subject to paradigm shifts that may cause the interpretation to be rebuilt from the ground up, but, this is as much of a strength of the seminar system as it is a weakness. The nature and conduct of the study group will be defined by the individual personalities that make up that group. Thus, the nature of the class, exploration, and development of skills will also be unpredictable. However, in the long run this approach produces much more knowledgeable theorists and capable teachers. They will have a greater understanding of the material, as they have been given the opportunity to tinker with and question it. They will be able to go beyond simply explaining the way things are done – they will be able to explain why they are done that way, and why they are not done another way.

This approach is not for everyone, nor should it necessarily replace the conventional paradigm – there is room enough for both. Students who desire clear leadership in their study will find the traditional paradigm more suitable, and, competitive fencers will also find the master-student system faster in developing the desired skills for competition. These personality types are not likely to present an issue, as they will tend to drift away from the slow pace of the seminar system. Nonetheless, these personalities will also come to a seminar-type group in order to change their approach or due to a lack of alternatives. It is important not to let the appearance of such personalities to overbear the more passive personalities in the group.

The overriding principle in seminar style training is consistency. The content and order of the practice remains the same from session to session. This doesn't mean that elements of the session do not progress; on the contrary, from a consistent base it becomes possible to cover a vast quantity of training in a fairly short amount of time. This consistency of training will permit the individual students to gain confidence in the system and to follow it under their own initiative. This confidence also will give the individual students agency in the process, and allow them to comment on the process and the material being studied. The other advantage of a process-driven seminar system is that individual members of the group will not miss out on specific information because they are absent from a class occasionally.

I provide an overview of my curriculum for running classes on Giganti. This tangible example should make the ideas discussed above clearer. This should also give a good starting place for the development of a curriculum for approaching the work of Nicoletto Giganti, or, most other fencing masters. I have used variations of this approach to teach students Ridolfo Capoferro, Fiore Dei Liberi, and the Lichtenhauer tradition. I encourage the reader to pick and choose what they like in the development of their own curriculum, and, to use other sources. I highly recommend Guy Windsor's *The Duellist's Companion* and William E. Wilson's *Arte of Defense* as sources for drills and exercises. I also encourage readers to contact me to discuss questions, ideas, and additions.

Each class is broken down into four parts:

    I.   Stretches
    II. Solo Drills
    III. Pair Drills
    IV. Free-play

There is no precise amount of time dedicated to each part of a practice. Rather each part is objective-based. In other words, there are a set type and number of stretches and solo drills to accomplish. This will be slow to start, but as the class members learn through repetition, the amount of time needed for these parts of the class will shorten considerably.

The less time taken by the first two parts of the class means the more time that can be utilized in the third and most important part of the class: the pair drills. During this part, the students will practice the individual plays covered in Giganti's work in order – or at least close to the order – presented in the book. Once again, this process will be slow to begin with, and there should not be the expectation to accomplish them all in in the first practice. Being able to run the entirety of Giganti's plays with the single sword, for instance, should take at least two or three dozen classes to achieve, and, there is no shame in taking longer than that.

Finally, when the students are deemed to be of sufficient skill, a portion of the class time should be dedicated to free play, so that students can attempt to put the lessons into practical use. The equipment required for free-play will be dependent on the organization under whose auspices you are practicing. If you are unaffiliated, it may be worthwhile investigating various Western Martial Arts (WMA) groups, the Historical European Martial Arts Alliance (HEMA Alliance), or The Society for Creative Anachronism (SCA). Any of these organizations may provide a local group to practice with, or at the very least provide safety and equipment guidelines to follow. Once again, Guy Windsor's *The Duellist's Companion* and William E. Wilson's *Arte of Defense* are also useful for providing advice on the topics of free play, safety, and equipment.

SAMPLE SYLLABUS

The following is the training system I use in my classes. Beginning with stretches and drills that have been found useful in conditioning students in Giganti's system of fencing. This is not considered a comprehensive list of possible warm-up exercises, nor are these stretches considered mandatory. Instructors should feel free to pick and choose their own stretches from this and other sources. However, whatever the curriculum, the instructor will find consistency in the order, content, and repetition of the stretches, warm-up, and drill beneficial. I have provided, in square brackets, the number of repetitions that I use to provide a starting place.

I. STRETCHES

Neck stretches

- Look up followed by look down: Standing with the feet parallel and comfortably shoulder-width apart, arms in a neutral position at the sides of the body, raise the chin to its extent. Then the chin is lowered toward the chest. [x3]

- Lean head forward with weight of the hands: Standing with the feet parallel and comfortably shoulder-width apart, the chin is lowered to the chest and the hands are placed on the back of the head in order to add weight to the stretch. The arms should not be used to pull the head, simply use the weight of the arms to extend the stretch. [x1]

- Lean left followed by lean right: Standing with the feet parallel and comfortably shoulder width apart, arms in a neutral position at the sides of the body, lower the right ear to the right shoulder. Then bring the head back to neutral and then lower the left ear to the left shoulder. [x3]

- Lean left and lean right with weight of the hand: This stretch is the same as the previous one. However, the arm on the side to which the head is being lowered is placed on the head to add extra weight to the stretch. The arm should not pull the head; simply use the weight of the arm to extend the stretch. [x1]

Arm Stretches

- Circling arms: Standing with the feet parallel and comfortably shoulder-width apart, with the arms held out from the sides parallel to the floor, start to circle the arms is small circles slowly getting bigger. When the circles are as large as they can possibly be, reverse direction and slowly make the circles smaller.

- Arm across body: Standing with the feet parallel and comfortably shoulder-width apart, extend a straightened arm across the body. With the forearm of the opposite arm, pull the straight arm in toward the body. Reverse the arms and repeat. [x3]

- Wrist stretches: Standing with the feet parallel and comfortably shoulder-width apart, the arms are held outstretched in front with the palms facing each other. The wrists are bent into each of four directions, in, up, out, and down. The wrists should then be turned through these positions in a circular fashion in both directions. [x1]

Torso Stretches

• Rib stretch: Standing with the feet parallel and comfortably shoulder-width apart, slide one hand down the leg on the same side. The other arm is bent over the body and head. Holding this position take several deep breaths. Switch and repeat on the opposite side. [x1]

• Torso rotations: Standing with the feet parallel and comfortably shoulder-width apart, ensure that both hips remain oriented forward, take one arm and reach to the rear on that side as far as possible. If the stretch in the ribs is not felt, then raise the arm as it is reaches to the rear. Repeat on the other side. [x3]

• Once that has been done, the exercise is repeated but this time with the body swung around as far as it will go. This will involve releasing the heel on the opposite side of the stretch and permitting the hips to twist with the torso. [x1]

Leg and Groin Stretches

• Crouch: Place feet in a comfortable position, roughly double-shoulder-width apart. Squat so that the knees are bent at a right angle or nearly so. Shift weight downward to stretch and lifting the backside to relax from the stretch, as needed. After stretching in the center-line, the weight should be moved to both left and right in order to stretch to each side. [x10]

• Calf Stretch and Knee to ground: Standing with the feet parallel and comfortably shoulder-width apart, take a deep step forward. Ensure the feet remain parallel to each other. Arch the back gently and bend the leading knee forward. This will stretch the front of the thigh and the calf of the trailing leg. Straighten the leading leg in order to relax the stretch, and repeat. After completing this part of the stretch, maintaining this stance the trailing knee is slowly brought down to the floor and then slowly brought back up. Repeat on the opposite side. [x1]

- Ankle Twists: Lifting one leg, the foot of the lifted leg will be rotated several times in both directions in order to loosen the ankle joint. [x3]

II. SOLO DRILLS

UNARMED DRILLS

I run my students through several conditioning drills in order to develop strength and flexibility in limbs and joints. Ideally, students will want to execute roughly 10 repetitions of the following exercises, although new students may will need to work up to that number. Typically, I have my students start with five repetitions for their first practice and then increase by one or two repetitions in each subsequent practice until the full twenty are reached. I have adopted several unarmed drills from Guy Windsor's system of training laid out in *The Duellist's Companion* and they are reproduced here with his permission.

- Squats: With the feet parallel and shoulder–width apart, and the arms held extended in front of the body, the body is lowered and then raised by bending the knees. Ideally, the legs will form a right angle at the knee. Slow steady motion is to be favoured over speed. [x10]

- Knee Bends: Assuming a proper stance with the weight supported by the bent back leg and almost no weight carried on the straight leading leg. The weight will then be transferred to the forward leg by straightening the back leg and bending the leading leg. Then the weight will be transferred to the back leg reversing the process. Bending the torso over the knee supporting the body's weight will help ease some of the supporting legs burden. I also periodically test my students standing in stance at various times, by asking them to pat their front foot on the ground to prove their weight is be held by the back leg. [x10]

- Torso Bends: In a proper stance with the weight supported the rear leg, lean the torso forward, taking care not to bend the forward knee or shift the weight. This will result in the rear buttock pushing toward the rear, this is perfectly normal. Then bend the torso back to the original position. [x10]

- Torso and Knee Bend: This combines the two previous drills. Bend the torso forward, followed by the knee bend forward. Then, bend the torso to the rear, followed by the knee bend to the rear.

- Torso and Knee Bends: Once the knee and torso bends have been practiced in isolation, the two exercises are combined to help students practice the proper movement of the body forward and backward. First, the torso is bent forward. Then the weight is brought forward by the knee bend. The student then bends the torso back followed by the weight of the body by the knee bend to the rear. Some of my students acknowledge the importance of this drill to the proper long under hand thrust by beginning the forward motion by extending the arm, and, retiring the arm back to a proper guard after the torso and knees have been bent to the rear.

- Footwork: In a proper stance conduct a number of forward and backward steps in both the inside and outside guards. [x20]

The biggest challenge in the interpretation of period instruction manuals is the reconstruction of the knowledge that the author assumed the reader possessed. This is also seen in the absent description of how one is to put their hand to the sword, as well as the plays that can be inferred from the text (see lesson 6, 11, and 28). Another obvious omission in Giganti, and indeed most other master's works, is footwork. The result is that the movement has to be reconstructed from the other information on stance and stepping available in the text. The following is one interpretation of how to step while remaining in a proper stance with the weight primarily on the back foot.

Forward: There are three distinct actions in the execution of a forward step, although the first is very hard to observe, and, it will seem that the first two occur simultaneously.

1) The pad of the inside foot behind the big toe (1st Metatarsal) is rolled forward (inverted), lifting the entire structure of the body and moving the body forward.

2) The outside foot is kicked forward on the heel and then rolled forward back in to place in order to continue the forward movement

3) The back foot then slides back into a proper stance.

Backward: There are also three distinct actions to a retiring step. Once again, the first and second actions seem to take place at the same time. In reality first phase precedes the second.

1) The inside foot is lifted and moved to its position in a proper stance at the end of the backward step.

2) The outside foot is rolled back onto the heel, moving the body upward and to the rear.

3) The outside foot then slides back to its position at the end of the step to for a proper stance.

WEAPON DRILLS

Once the stretches and the unarmed drills have been completed, the students put on gloves and take their weapons in hand for a series of technique and strengthening drills.

Rolling: This is a series of exercises that are meant to increase arm strength and to make students more comfortable with the movement of the sword. This series of exercises are conducted with the sword first in the outside and then the inside guard positions. These drills can be done in a proper stance or with a more relaxed footing. It is imperative that the student begin and end in a proper inside and outside guard.

Outside Guard:

• Rolling Up: From the starting position, the wrist is bent backwards, bringing the sword upwards and towards the rear, then the momentum of the sword carries it backwards and falling in a circular motion back, then down, and finally to the front. The wrist will be turned in order to permit the sword to continue in its circular fashion and to bring it back

into a proper guard. [x10]

- Rolling Down: By turning the palm of the hand up, the sword begins its movement downward and to the outside, and finally to the rear. When the sword reaches the rear, the wrist is turned over again and the sword will come back to guard. [x10]

- Rolling Out (Circling): This is the action of circling of the sword. The palm of the hand is turned sharply up into the inside guard position and sharply returned to the outside guard. It is important that the blade is dragged by this motion and not forced from side to side by the movement of the hand. The tip of the sword is to describe a circle. [x10]

- Counter Circle: This roll is similar in motion to rolling out (described above). However, rather than ending in a proper guard, the fencer ends with their sword arm retracted, the tip of the sword point upward, and moved further to the outside of the body. After pausing in this position briefly, the fencer returns the sword to a proper guard. [x10]

Inside Guard:

- Rolling Up: The hand is turned over to the rear and the sword will follow the upward and then rear movement of the hand. As the sword's momentum carries the sword downward and then forward, the wrist will be turned back into the proper guard position. [x10]

- Rolling Down: This movement is in reality more to the side than down. Once again, the hand is turned over to the rear as the sword moves downward slightly and out to the inside, the motion of the hand back into proper position is completed by turning the palm up, back into guard. [x10]

- Rolling in (Circling): The opposite of rolling out. This is the action of the circling of the sword in the inside guard. The hand is turned sharply into the outside guard position and then sharply returned to the inside guard. It is important that the blade is dragged by this motion and not forced from side to side by the movement of the hand. The tip of the sword is to describe a circle. [x10]

- Counter Circle: This roll is similar in motion to rolling in (described above). However, rather than ending in a proper guard, the fencer should end with their sword arm retracted, the tip of the sword point more upward than normal, and moved significantly to the inside of the body. After pausing in this position briefly, the fencer should return the sword to an inside guard. [x10]

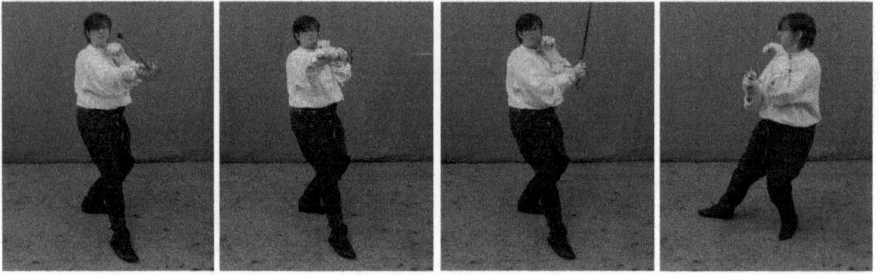

- Long Under hand thrust: Against a target or into the air, practice throwing a number of outside long underhand points. Then throw an equal number of under hand thrusts from the inside guard. [x30 in each guard]

III. PAIR DRILLS, OR PLAYS

One of the key elements of training is repetition. This is true not only of specific techniques, but also of the tactics of the fight. Just like with specific techniques, drilling Giganti's plays consistently will give an instinctive ability to use his tactical concepts during the pressure of free play. Constant repetition also permits continuing refinement of a fencer's own skills and understanding of Giganti's work by providing frequent opportunities to revisit the plays.

The plays should be practiced in a consistent order. Giganti's book, with a few revisions, is laid out in a fairly good order for practicing the plays. How far through the plays a class will get is not defined and the students will progress as far as possible, given available time and attention span. The first time the play is studied it should be practiced with each participant performing the technique 10 or 20 times to their satisfaction. Once this is done, a play has been considered to have been introduced. An introduced play will then be practiced three times by each participant in subsequent practices, with new plays being introduced as the students work their way through the plays each practice.

The following are the single sword plays and the order that my students practice them:

1) Simple Bind
2) Circling against a bind (lesson 8)
3) Warding against a Circling (lesson 6 and 7)
4) Counter Circle (lesson 9 and 10)
5) Feint (lesson 11 and 12)

6) Feint in distance (lesson 13)
7) Feint raising the sword (lesson 14)
8) Outside passage with a feint (lesson 15)
9) Passage with the Sword with both hands (lesson 17)
10) Inquartata (lessons 19, 20, and 21)
11) Affronting the sword (lesson 22)
12) Parry of a thrust to the chest (lesson 24)
13) Turning the wrist (lesson 25)

IV. CLASS/FREEPLAY

It is useful to ensure that when conducting freeplay each student plays a set number of bouts (three to five seems to be a good number) with every other student in the class at single sword, and then sword and dagger if they are studying it. This ensures that students are given the opportunity to apply the skills developed in training against as wide a variety of opponents. This will also prevent the drilled skills from becoming too rigid.

About the Translator

AARON MIEDEMA HAS taken a crooked path to arrive at this book. He began his aspirations as a thespian in 1990, studying a B.F.A. in Theatre Studies at York University. He put this schooling to good use in founding and running the Renaissance Stage Company in Kingston, Ontario, between 1992 and 2000.

During his time in the theatre that he developed an interest in stage combat and historical martial arts, and after 2000 he began to dedicate himself to the study and practice of ancient and historical fencing. He was introduced to the work of Nicoletto Giganti by Gary Chelack in 2002, and, began his own translation of *Scola overò Teatro*...a year later.

In 2005, he returned to school, attending Carleton University in Ottawa to pursue studies in Italian, Latin, and the social history of late medieval and early modern Europe. With this knowledge, Aaron began the translation and interpretation of other Italian martial artists of the fifteenth, sixteenth, and seventeenth centuries. At Carleton University Aaron also met Dr. Tim Cook, who focused these martial interests into the study of the role of close combat and Bayonet Fighting in tactical doctrine of the Great War. This became the subject of his Master's thesis in the Department of War Studies at the Royal Military College of Canada. His thesis became his first book, *Bayonets and Blobsticks: The Canadian Experience of Close Combat 1915-18* (2011).

This detour into the study of the Great War led to other opportunities for Aaron. He put his theatrical and historical knowledge to good use in his role as Historical Advisor, Set Designer, and Actor in the feature film *21 Brothers* (2011). The film is set in the trenches just before the Battle of Fleurs-Courcelette in September 1916. It is also the Guinness World Record holder for "longest film shot in a single take."

Aaron has returned to academia, and is now in his second year of his Ph.D. at York University. His studies have turned from the early twentieth century back to the sixteenth. His research focuses on the legal and cultural place of the duel in Late Renaissance Italy. After more than twenty years, it is somewhat perplexing that he is only two buildings over and one floor up from where he started his academic career.

He currently resides in Scarborough, Ontario, with his partner Yvonne.

Also Available from Legacy Books Press

Bayonets and Blobsticks: The Canadian Experience of Close Combat 1915-1918

By Aaron Taylor Miedema

ISBN: 978-0-9784652-9-2

For a long time, it has been accepted that the bayonet was an inadequate weapon in World War I – an anachronism, relied upon by foolish generals eager to relive the glories of the Napoleonic Wars while incapable of coming to terms with the modern battlefield and trench warfare. But was this the reality of the Western Front of the Great War, or a myth perpetuated by historians?

In reality, the soldiers of World War I seemed oblivious to what appears so obvious to critics ninety years removed. They quite liked their bayonets, and they used them – often.

In this fascinating and provocative study, Aaron Taylor Miedema takes a new look at the role of the bayonet and shock tactics on the Western front. Through the experience of the Canadian Corps – the British shock troops of the Western Front – he challenges the conventional view of the bayonet as an obsolete weapon system and rekindles the controversial debate over technologies, old and new, on the field of battle.